BIG POTATOES:
THE LONDON MANI
FOR INNOVATION

CONTENTS

PREFACE TO THE SECOND EDITION — 7

1. THINK BIG — 17
Defining innovation and its potential
Scale is beautiful

2. GO BEYOND THE POST-WAR LEGACY OF INNOVATION — 20
The re-animation of frozen corpses
Argricultural, first and second industrial revolutions
What's up, Doc?

3. PRINCIPLES, NOT MODELS — 25
The same old tilts at the old, linear model
Models as substitutes for technological innovation

4. IN PRAISE OF 'USELESS' RESEARCH — 29
From progress to expediency
Retrieving the arguments for basic research

5. INNOVATION IS HARD WORK — 32
In innovation, there's no such thing as a free lunch
Innovation is an uphill struggle

6. FOR SUCCESS, EXPECT LOTS OF FAILURES — 35
Failure cannot be avoided

7. REGARD CHANCE AND SURPRISE AS ALLIES — 38
As human endeavours, innovation and technology will surprise
Let's hear it for unanticipated needs

8. TAKE RISKS — 41
Innovation is risky. Get over it
Conscious innovation is the best way to deal with risks

9. INNOVATION DEMANDS LEADERSHIP 45
Restating the case for leaders
The innovator as hero

10. INNOVATION IS EVERYBODY'S RESPONSIBILITY 49
The who of innovation
Innovation as new organisation
The role of design and branding

11. TRUST THE PEOPLE, NOT REGULATION 53
Lessons of Copenhagen
Regulations that haven't helped
Greeted by popular and professional acclaim

12. THINK GLOBAL, ACT GLOBAL 58
Place is overrated
The space for innovation
Slums as an example to follow

13. THE SPIRIT OF INNOVATION KNOWS NO LIMITS 63
A narrowed scope for innovation: the example of climatology
Resource depletion and the depletion of the human spirit
Why innovation knows no end
Markets, sticks, carrots and nudges are no substitute

14. BY, WITH, AND FOR HUMANITY 70
By humanity
With humanity
For humanity

ABOUT THE AUTHORS 76

HOW WE'RE CAMPAIGNING FOR INNOVATION 79

Photo: Cladding is fitted to the East Coast Mainline bridge that will allow Eurostar trains to cross tracks going into Kings Cross station, London

PREFACE TO THE SECOND EDITION

Since it was published in January 2010, the Big Potatoes manifesto has created a growing international circle of enthusiasts. More and more people recognise that today's rhetoric about innovation has yet to be matched by reality. That's why Big Potatoes has been published in Germany, [1] and why we hope to publish in China, too.

Looking at Innovation and its Impediments on a sector-by-sector basis, supporters of Big Potatoes have formed workgroups on

◊ ICT [2]
◊ Art [3]
◊ Design [4]
◊ Cities and transport [5]
◊ Energy [6]
◊ Media. [7]

These workgroups have begun to build up a picture of innovation all over the world. By contrast, this Preface to the second English edition concentrates on British developments — in particular, those emerging around the issues now being reviewed by Big Potatoes workgroups.

Britain's Conservative and Liberal-Democrat coalition issued a political programme straight after it was formed in May 2010. [8] Though it was always likely to be overtaken by events, that programme still provides a useful snapshot of the wider drift that characterises innovation in the West today.

HOW BRITAIN'S COALITION GOVERNMENT RESPONDS TO INNOVATION CHALLENGES IN ICT — AND THE ARTS

Here's how often the Coalition programme, which runs to more than 30 pages, mentions some key words:

Mentions in the Coalition programme:

Computers, Telecommunications, ICT	2
Art, the arts, culture beyond media and sport	2
Design	0
Cities	1
Transport, Energy	one section on each issue — see below
Science	4
Research	5
Innovation	8
Technology	8
Spending	**17**
Taxation	**39**

Of the two mentions of ICT, one is about publishing government ICT contracts online; the other, about enabling large government ICT projects to be split into smaller bits. There's no hint that ICT might improve productivity, economic growth or the quality of life.

Spending, taxes, incomes, bonuses, pensions, prices, who owns what, and where: these things, not innovation, now dominate worldwide debates on economic policy. In Britain, some go out of their way to attack the City of London, uphold Manufacturing, or praise Happiness. Science and technological innovation, however, are just taken for granted. In a single outing for the word 'digital', the Coalition says that it will 'consider' using

> 'the part of the TV licence fee that is supporting the digital switchover [of TVs in 2012] to fund broadband in areas that the market alone will not reach'.

Now, household ownership of TVs has exceeded 93 per cent in Britain since 1989-90. One might therefore think that to convert, in 2012, all those TVs to handle digital broadcasting is a key challenge for innovation. One might also think that the advent of full Internet services to TVs is, like broadband, another key challenge for innovation. But switching funds from one technology to another seems to fascinate officialdom much more than getting all the best ICT actually adopted. Though the media obsess about the iPhone, elites just don't seem very interested either in creating a broader political and cultural climate in support of innovation, or in seeing innovation through.

Policy on the arts presents the same story of accounting and auditing, not innovation. The Coalition programme proclaims that entry to museums will remain free, which is welcome. For the rest, however, we are simply told that reform of the National Lottery may give the arts more money.

Now of course, governments cannot and should not decree what the course of innovation in the arts should be. But in both the arts and ICT, just some imaginative engagement with innovation would help people identify red herrings, clarify goals, set agendas, and — not least — determine what kind of <u>content</u> these milieux might properly look forward to in future.

PLANS FOR DESIGN, CITIES AND TRANSPORT

All is not lost. Take, for example, design. Despite the entry of new players in the field (naturally, including China and India), Britain's reputation in design is still quite high.

Maintaining that reputation, however, is something that, like the related task of pursuing urban revival in a climate of parsimony, invites <u>leadership</u> in innovation — Principle 9 of this manifesto. Where is that leadership? Unhappily, the only passage in the Coalition programme remotely relating either to design or to urban revival is about the creation of directly elected mayors in England's 12 largest cities. No doubt this is all very democratic; but the <u>substantive new policies and substantive new technologies</u> that might bring real dynamism to design and to cities are nowhere discussed.

The Coalition programme tries harder on transport. Of course, it nods at greener and more sustainable systems, and at tougher regulations on emissions. Still, about the railways there is at least a call for better services, stations and trains, as well as a commitment to a truly national high-speed rail network — achieved, predictably enough, 'in phases'.

That, however, is nearly all that the Coalition programme has to say about transport. It favours a national recharging system for electric and plug-in hybrid vehicles, but will brook no new aircraft runways at Heathrow, Gatwick or Stansted. New or better roads do not figure in its perspective: instead, innovation in transport is much more about the need for... more cycling and walking.

ENERGY: PLENTY OF REGULATION, NOT MUCH R&D

Principle 11 of this <u>Big Potatoes</u> enjoins readers to trust the people, not regulation. That's relevant to innovation in energy.

◊ in 2009, the average time taken for any kind of wind turbine to gain planning approval in Britain was 15 months. Local authority approvals for wind turbines had fallen from 68 per cent in 2008 to 53 per cent [9]

◊ in 2010, British industry gave up on a tidal energy scheme for the Severn, fearful that to get planning permission might cost it £250m.[10]

Apart from slowing up energy innovation with bureaucracy, the British state slows it up by inept financial moves. One of the Coalition's first acts was to cancel an £80m loan to Sheffield Forgemasters. That loan was to finance the installation of a forging press with which to challenge Japan Steel in giant steel forgings for nuclear reactors.

At the end of the Coalition programme section on energy, Tories and Lib-Dems agree to disagree about nuclear power. But in practice, at Sheffield, they have already united to stop innovation in nuclear engineering.

Nobody in the Coalition would like to admit to what is happening in energy innovation. UK state support for research, development and deployment (RD&D) in energy, for instance, isn't just low, but embarrassingly low. For every £10,000 Britain generates in Gross Domestic Product (GDP), Whitehall spares just £1 on researching how to keep the lights on:

State spending on energy RD&D as a percentage of GDP, 2007 [11]

Japan, Finland	nearly 0.09
Korea	more than 0.05
France	0.05
Denmark	nearly 0.05
Norway	0.04
US, Italy	nearly 0.03
Germany	nearly 0.02
UK	**0.01**
Spain	under 0.01
Ireland	about 0.005

In fact state support for RD&D in energy is low right around the world: the International Energy Agency, for example, estimates that public support for energy RD&D around the world should be multiplied by between two and five times. [12] But in Britain as elsewhere, research into energy by business is nothing to celebrate either:

Percentage of sales revenues spent on energy R&D by companies among the largest 1000 firms in the UK, 2008/9, by sector [13]

Electricity	0.2
Gas, water & multi-utilities	0.1
Oil and gas producers	0.2

Of course, in energy as in any other sector, simply increasing budgets for R&D does not guarantee successful innovation. But these statistics provide ample grounds for concern. Since the disaster of Deepwater Horizon, BP has attracted a lot of attention. Perhaps BP might not be where it is now, had it spent more than £2 in every £1000 it earned on researching and developing the future. [14]

We can be sure that we won't be hearing much about any of this from the Coalition.

THE NEW DUPLICITY IN SCIENCE AND INNOVATION

In September 2010, Dr Vincent Cable, minister in charge of the Department of Business Innovation and Skills, announced that he was in favour of 'blue skies' research in science, but also that he wanted to 'screen out' what he called 'mediocrity' among British scientists. [15] How should we take this posture?

In the Coalition programme, one mention of science calls for 'a carefully managed and science-led policy of badger control in areas with high and persistent levels of bovine tuberculosis'. Another is about teaching science; another about reducing the use of animals in scientific research; a fourth is about maintaining Sites of Special Scientific Interest.

With this kind of treatment of science, it is hard to take seriously Dr Cable's professed fondness for open-ended, world-beating science — even if we leave aside Whitehall's continuing efforts to subject higher education and science to cuts in state expenditure. In its eight mentions of innovation, the Coalition programme betrays a similar insouciance. Two mentions go on innovation (especially that in ICT) allowing the government, in a rather ominous manner, to extend 'transparency' to 'every area' of public life. The programme also wants those Non-Governmental Organisations dealing with overseas poverty to be smaller and more innovative. It wants Britain to export green technologies. And it says it wants innovation in economy, business and society.

Inspiring stuff. In fact what is really meant by 'innovation', here as elsewhere, is well captured by a passing phrase that is made in the Coalition's passage on public health. What is needed, it says, is an 'ambitious strategy' which harnesses 'innovative techniques to help people take responsibility for their own health'.

The chief conceit about innovation today is here laid bare. Innovation is not about science, technology, laboratories, curiosity, experiment, prototypes, generating new needs or anything like that. Termed 'social' innovation, it is really about innovation in behaviour. [16] Overpaid bankers must make innovations in their behaviour. Men with too much testosterone must do the same. Here, any amount of blue skies thinking is suddenly permissible, as long as liberties are curbed, individuals start to behave themselves, and science and technology are ignored.

Since 2008, when the US economists Richard Thaler and Cass Sunstein published Nudge: improving decisions about health, wealth, and happiness, the idea has grown that the state's job is to act as a paternalistic 'choice architect', guiding feckless and irrational people to the right path. [17] Conservative leader David Cameron took up this doctrine almost immediately. [18] Today, every initiative in fields such as transport or energy can only be made, officials say, by first recognising that technology is 'not the only answer' (whoever said it was?). Then, in the usual condescending style, it's suggested that 'helping people make informed choices' about their behaviour – that is, dutifully accepting the choice laid down from on high – does, in fact, amount to the only answer.

This is cheap, in every sense of the word.

www.bigpotatoes.org

CONCLUSION

Torpor and duplicitous rhetoric in innovation are not trends confined to Britain: they are all too easy to notice elsewhere.

Of course, there are steps forward in science and technology. One example is that, more than 10 years after two of the world's most acclaimed thinkers announced the advent of the biotech century, [19] there are modest signs of progress.

Like other sectors, medicine is making some advances. Several pharmaceutical firms, for example, raised their R&D expenditure in the teeth of the recession, 2008-9. [20] However, a worldwide survey of 2240 corporate executives, performed by McKinsey in 2010 and running across a full range of industries, regions, functional specialties and seniority, confirms some familiar problems with innovation in business.

Among the respondents, 55 per cent have, since 2008, said that their companies are better than their peers at innovation — but far fewer now say their companies are good at generating breakthrough ideas, selecting the right ones, prototyping, and developing business cases for innovation. Only 26 per cent say their firms were good at stopping ideas at the right time; only 27 per cent say their firms are very or extremely effective at making their leaders formally accountable for innovation. About 40 per cent of respondents say their companies make decisions on commercialising innovations in an ad hoc manner; only 23 per cent are sure that such decisions are a regular topic at top meetings. An astonishing 57 per cent say that though their employers 'execute well on the few good ideas we have', they need 'a more robust pipeline of big ideas'. [21]

For all Britain's supposedly unique record of amateurism in innovation, McKinsey underlines how lack of formal organisation characterises the world's corporate efforts in this domain. Of course, the executives polled say they prefer to make new products, services or customers than to engage in mergers and acquisitions (M&A). But in 2010, M&A in the ICT sector, like M&A designed to access new geographical markets, has — not for the first time — emerged as more or less a distraction from the far messier business of making fundamental breakthroughs in science and technology.

With plastic electronics and photonics, there is forward movement. But recent takeovers made by Intel, Oracle and Hewlett-Packard reveal industry consolidation, not Joseph Schumpeter's creative destruction. With President Obama's state takeover of General Motors, we saw neither creation nor destruction. Reinforcing that picture, the total number of patent applications filed at the patent offices of nine key countries decreased by 2.9 per cent, 2008-9. Here is a breakdown of the statistics:

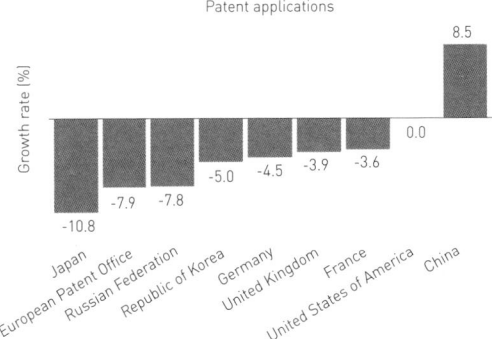

Applications for patents, 2008-9: rates of growth, selected countries [22]

Clearly the world can expect to see some important innovations coming out of China. In ICT between 2008 and 2009, for example, Microsoft and Apple increased their R&D spending by a creditable 10 and 20 per cent, respectively, but China's Huawei and ZTE raised theirs by an impressive 27 and 45 per cent.

On average and around the world, however, publicly listed firms cut spending on R&D by 1.7 per cent, 2008-9. Most automotive firms spent less (General Motors, down 24.5 per cent; Toyota, down 19.8 per cent). So did firms in construction (Caterpillar, down 17.8 per cent), and in consumer products (Unilever, down 3.9 per cent).

The problem that Big Potatoes seeks to address isn't just that innovation is too often an informal business in the West. The problem isn't even that declining corporate profitability and rising state indebtedness each make serious spending on R&D look too risky. No, the problem is that innovation has largely dropped out of the West's intellectual purview. It certainly doesn't form a central part of the West's political and economic toolbox any more. Indeed European Union research commissioner Máire Geoghegan-Quinn has warned of an 'innovation emergency' [23], so weak has Europe's commitment to R&D become.

Perhaps, in Britain, there will be a whole lot more rhetoric about innovation from the Coalition. David Cameron himself has discovered that capital projects such as high-speed rail, or carbon capture and storage schemes for power stations, are very good for long-term UK competitiveness. At the Department for Business Innovation and Skills, the charismatic Dr Vincent Cable is supposed to favour something like the local 'Clerk Maxwell Centres' for Technology and Innovation proposed to Lord Mandelson in the dying days of the last government [24].

Well, civil service press releases about UK innovation may increase, just as state budgets for innovation may rise in absolute terms. Yet compared to all the challenges for innovation that like ahead, real, continuous and inspired commitment to innovation will demand more than bigger budgets, whether public or private. For innovation to become a truly informed part of everyday discussion and everyday business, an intellectual and cultural revolution will be necessary.

That will not be achieved easily. As Daniel Ben-Ami has pointed out, a 'Yes, but!' scepticism about economic growth dominates Western discourse nowadays [25]. Similarly, nearly every enlightened authority now takes the view that science and technology bring major hazards in their wake [26].

In fact, however, science and technology have always brought hazard with them. Yet not so very long after humankind created fire, it began to develop ways of putting fires out.

Right now, we could all do with a lot more fire in the realm of innovation.

James Woudhuysen, October 2010

References:

[1] < http://www.novo-argumente.com/magazin.php/dfa/artikel/big_potatoes/ >

[2] < http://www.bigpotatoes.org/ict >

[3] < http://www.bigpotatoes.org/art >

[4] < http://www.bigpotatoes.org/design >

[5] < http://www.audacity.org/250-New-Towns-index.htm >

[6] < http://www.bigpotatoes.org/energy >

[7] < http://www.bigpotatoes.org/media >

[8] The Coalition: our programme for government, May 2010, on < http://www.cabinetoffice.gov.uk/media/409088/pfg_coalition.pdf >.

[9] Climate Change Committee, Building a low-carbon economy — the UK's innovation challenge, July 2010, p24, on < http://downloads.theccc.org.uk.s3.amazonaws.com/Low%20carbon%20Innovation/CCC_Low-Carbon_WEB.pdf >. The statutory target for planning approval of wind turbines is 16 weeks for on-shore devices.

[10] Declan Lynch, 'Planning costs may pull the plug on Severn Barrage', Business Green, 9 September 2010.

[11] Climate Change Committee, op cit, p22.

[12] Cited in ibid, p21.

[13] Department for Business Innovation & Skills, The 2009 R&D Scoreboard: the top 1,000 UK and 1,000 global companies by R&D investment — company data, March 2010, pp 10, 18, 28, on < http://www.innovation.gov.uk/rd_scoreboard/downloads/2009_RD_Scoreboard_Final.pdf >. Among large oil equipment, services and distribution firms based in the UK,

what is termed R&D intensity is a more respectable 2.1 per cent, though these firms are dwarfed in size by primary producers of oil and gas.

[14] Figure from ibid, p28. The R&D intensity of Royal Dutch Shell is better than that of BP: it stands not at 0.2 per cent, but at 0.3.

[15] Cable, 'Science, Research and Innovation', speech, 8 September 2010, on < http://www.bis.gov.uk/news/speeches/vince-cable-science-research-and-innovation-speech >.

[16] See 'Social innovation: Let's hear those ideas', The Economist, 12 August 2010, on < http://www.economist.com/node/16789766?story_id=16789766&fsrc=rss >.

[17] Richard Thaler and Cass Sunstein, Nudge: improving decisions about health, wealth, and happiness, Yale University Press, 2008.

[18] David Cameron, 'The power of social innovation', speech, 13 June 2008, on < http://www.conservatives.com/News/Speeches/2008/06/David_Cameron_The_power_of_social_innovation.aspx >.

[19] See Jeremy Rifkin, The biotech century: the coming age of genetic commerce, Weidenfeld & Nicolson, 1998; Francis Fukuyama, Our posthuman future: consequences of the biotechnology revolution, Profile Books, 2002.

[20] World Intellectual Property Organization (WIPO), 'Signs of Recovery Emerge after Economic Crisis Hits Innovation & IP Filings', Press release, 15 September 2010, on < http://www.wipo.int/pressroom/en/articles/2010/article_0029.html >. The report on which this press release was based, World Intellectual Property Indicators 2010, September 2010, is on < http://www.wipo.int/export/sites/www/ipstats/en/statistics/patents/pdf/941e_2010.pdf >.

[21] McKinsey, Innovation and commercialization, 2010: McKinsey Global Survey results, August 2010, on < https://www.mckinseyquarterly.com/Innovation_and_commercialization_2010_McKinsey_Global_Survey_results_2662 >.

[22] WIPO, op cit, Figure 2: Patent and Trademark Applications Growth Rate (2008-09).

[23] Nikki Tait, 'Brussels warns of "innovation emergency"', Financial Times, 5 October 2010, on < http://www.ft.com/cms/s/0/173ef6d8-d09c-11df-8667-00144feabdc0.html >.

[24] On Cameron, see George Parker and Jane Croft, 'Cameron orders good news plan amid cuts', Financial Times, 1 October 2010, on < http://www.ft.com/cms/s/0/e773f5c2-cd8d-11df-9c82-00144feab49a.html >. Innovation centres are recommended in Hermann Hauser, The Current and Future Role of Technology and Innovation Centres in the UK, 2010, on < http://www.bis.gov.uk/assets/biscore/innovation/docs/10-843-role-of-technology-innovation-centres-hauser-review >.

[25] Daniel Ben-Ami, Ferraris for all: in defence of economic progress, Policy Press, 2010.

[26] See for example Nicholas Carr, The shallows: what the Internet is doing to our brains, W. W. Norton & Company, 2010.

PHOTO: The east deck of St Pancras International station on 12 April 2004, the day it opened for domestic train services

#1
THINK BIG

The full entry of China and India into the world economy doesn't just mean billions more consumers aspiring to Western lifestyles. It also means that the world can benefit from billions of innovating brains. It's a moment to broaden horizons, expect much more, and expand every kind of ambition.

First, though, Britain and the West need to recover a sense of what innovation is and just how much it can do.

DEFINING INNOVATION AND ITS POTENTIAL

Innovation cannot be reduced to technology: while it embraces improvements both in process and in product or service, these often accompany changes in organisation.[1] However today technological innovation is weak in private services, weaker still in public services, and takes second place to changes in business model — different ways of taking money from customers. In particular, business expenditure on research and development (R&D), taken as a fraction of GDP, has been stagnant in America and Europe for 15 years or more. [2] In that faltering context, where the Organization for Economic Cooperation and Development talks up what it calls 'the central importance of non technological innovation', [3] it's essential to uphold the powerful improvements, above all in productivity, that new techniques can bring.

When Adam Smith published The wealth of nations in 1776, he didn't know that the title to his famous passage, 'The division of labour in pin manufacturing (and the great increase in the quantity of work that results)' would be on the back of every £20 note. Nor could he have realised how much bigger, with China and India, is the stock of ingenuity that mankind can now mobilise. [4] Yet today all corners of the Earth can rightly hope to move on toward a global division of labour far in advance of what we can imagine. By itself, that won't lead to more time for leisure or more equality. But with more than one billion people going hungry for the first time in 40 years, [5] the need for productivity step-changes just in agriculture, irrigation and food distribution has seldom been greater.

In innovation there can be no skipping over the need for professional expertise. Still, with the opening up of Asia, more people can now specialise more deeply in particular lines of work — something that will also allow multidisciplinary initiatives in innovation to be more successful. The Internet and machine translation make international collaboration easier. So, after all today's ignorance about the whereabouts of toxic assets, the world now has a chance finally to move toward the much vaunted, prematurely announced 'knowledge economy'.

SCALE IS BEAUTIFUL

Of course, Britain will not make digital cameras any time soon. Conversely, China will not forever build coal-fired power stations unequipped with carbon capture and storage. But between the nations of the world there is now an opening to share profound insights, agree on vaulting objectives, and take wealth to a qualitatively higher level: to provide more growth, and a better kind of growth.

The first principle of a new, innovatory global division of labour for the 21st century is that scale is beautiful, not smallness. In mobile telephony and electronics, miniaturisation has its place; but to lower the cost of handsets enough for the world's poor to be able to afford them, still larger, more automated production lines are needed. To make the most of sources of renewable energy, which are very diffuse, demands scale undertakings, not David Cameron's kind of roof-mounted home windmill. Even without attacking the world's deteriorated and substandard housing, UN estimates suggest, the world must build no fewer than 4000 houses an hour — if its increasing population is to be housed and its slums replaced. [6] More than a third of a century after Ernst Schumacher's Small is beautiful (1973), it's time to wave goodbye to humility, parochialism, and the dogma of 'act local'.

Innovation must set its sights high, and can never do things by halves. Innovation is, at its best, Big Potatoes.

References:

[1] In the classic account of the Austrian economist Joseph Schumpeter, 'long-term improvements in output and cheapness' came from new technologies and methods of production or transport, but also from new consumer goods, new markets, new sources of supply and new forms of organisation. See Joseph Schumpeter, Capitalism, Socialism and Democracy (1942), Unwin Paperbacks, 1987.

[2] See Organization for Economic Cooperation and Development (OECD), Main Science and Technology Indicators (MSTI): 2009-1, 13 July 2009, on < http://www.oecd.org/dataoecd/9/44/41850733.pdf >.

[3] OECD, Policy Responses to the Economic Crisis: Investing in Innovation for Long-Term Growth, June 2009, p16, on < http://www.oecd.org/dataoecd/59/45/42983414.pdf >.

[4] On top of the populous East, a mere billion people in the West now have, in their leisure time and their widespread access to the Web, an opportunity to volunteer to collaborate on innovation for between two and six billion hours a day. See Yochai Benkler, The Wealth of Networks: How Social Production Transforms Markets and Freedom, Yale University Press, 2006, p55.

[5] United Nations, The State of Food Insecurity in the World 2009, October 2009, on < ftp://ftp.fao.org/docrep/fao/012/i0876e/i0876e.pdf >.

[6] Figure derived from United Nations Human Settlements Programme, Financing Urban Shelter – Global Report on Human Settlements 2005, 2005, Tables 1.2 and 1.3, p5, on < http://www.unhabitat.org/pmss/getElectronicVersion.asp?nr=1818&alt=1 >.

#2
GO BEYOND THE POST-WAR LEGACY OF INNOVATION

Experts on innovation always agree that it is speeding up 'exponentially'. But is that true?

In 1965, in just four pages, the later co-founder of Intel, Gordon Moore, noted that the 'complexity for minimum component costs' of integrated circuits — that is, the number of transistors per chip that yielded the minimum cost per transistor — had roughly doubled each year from 1962 to 1965. Though he hardly needed to say so, that pattern is an exponential one. Still, Moore added that there was no reason to believe that it would not remain nearly constant for at least another 10 years. [1]

Moore's extrapolation, however valid, is no unbending law of the future of the whole of electronics. To extend it beyond electronics is still less permissible. Innovation in pharmaceuticals, for example, is slowing. [2]

When boosters of IT rave about exponential growth, they should really say 'accelerating, but only for the moment'. [3] While we wouldn't rule out everyone owning five mobile phones, exponential growth tends, more rapidly than linear growth, to move toward infinity. And right now, the world's technological growth is not tending toward infinity. Indeed since the West re-encountered economic crises in the early 1970s, the US in particular has had a kind of secret crisis of innovation, despite all the technological advances it has undeniably registered. [4]

THE RE-ANIMATION OF FROZEN CORPSES

The US inventor-forecaster Ray Kurzweil believes that disease-fighting micro-robots in the human body, artificial intelligence, and the reanimation of frozen corpses are technologies that will move in such an exponential style, they will transform life 'irreversibly' by 2045. [5] Yet technologies much less exotic than these always irreversibly transform life: the breakfast cereal, for example, cannot easily be dis-invented. Yes, the diffusion of the endlessly cited iPhone is faster than that of domestic appliances in the 1920s. But the development of the Internet-enabled mobile phone has taken decades — and in genetics, James Watson, Francis Crick and Rosalind Franklin first published on the structure of DNA back in 1953. [6]

Perhaps people think that innovation is accelerating because they feel they have little control over their lives. Yet while earlier surges of innovation embraced a whole range of sectors, today's advances don't quite do that. It's time for something better.

AGRICULTURAL, FIRST AND SECOND INDUSTRIAL REVOLUTIONS

In Britain the agricultural revolution embraced Jethro Tull's mechanical seed drill (1701), Joseph Foljambe's patented, lightweight, iron-fitted Rotherham Plough (1730, bought by George Washington and eventually factory-made), and Andrew Meikle's grain threshing machine of the 1780s. It took in Flemish crop rotation, Flemish hydrology, and the selective breeding of animals. By raising productivity on the land, the agricultural revolution made cheap food and a surplus population of workers available for the first industrial revolution.

That began with the manufacture of wool (Kay's fly-shuttle, 1733), and improved productivity in garment manufacture. Finished cloth was bleached with sulphuric acid and chlorine, and patterned with cylindrical printing. Downtimes in mills fell as components and frames came to be made of iron, leather belts replaced pulley-ropes, and gearing and shafting were rationalised. Blast furnaces turned out iron at high levels of purity, and, unlike mills and windmills, steam engines worked year-round. They modernised coal mining; and, with the commercial application, after 1776, of James Watt's improvement on Thomas Newcomen's steam engine (1705), the science of thermodynamics took off. The design, precision and smooth operation of metalworking tools improved and, with that, the standardisation of bolts and screws. [7] Britain's James Brindley pioneered canal building; America's Benjamin Franklin hit upon the wood-burning stove and lightning conductor, and France's Joseph Marie Jacquard devised, about 1800, punched cards to control the weaving of silk.

Spanning the decades around 1900, the second industrial revolution included electric power and motors, organic chemistry and synthetics, the internal combustion engine and automotive devices, precision manufacture and assembly-line production. [8] Steel, petrochemicals, printing and papermaking, lighting and vacuum tubes and cathode ray tubes, packaged goods, soaps and cleaners, cameras and film cameras, surgery and anaesthesia: all these advanced dramatically. So did the railways. There emerged mechanical typesetting, mechanical refrigeration, diesel locomotives, electric trolley cars, steel ships, modern submarines, chain-driven bicycles, gyrocompasses, safety razors, department stores, radio and the telephone. [9] Herman Hollerith's tabulating machine assisted in the first US Census (1890), laying the basis for IBM. [10] In December 1903 the Wright Brothers performed their first powered flights, and in 1912 the discovery of Bakelite was announced. To control the flow of goods brought about by steam-powered factories and locomotives, typewriters and telegraphs multiplied. [11]

WHAT'S UP, DOC?

Previous waves of innovation, then, were international, and prefigured some of what we now know as IT. Importantly, they coincided with major social, economic and political upheavals, and new hopes in the possibility and necessity of progress. In that context, the first and second 'industrial' revolutions were wide-ranging, more or less conscious attempts to save heaps of time in production processes.

After 1939 things were a little different. Many innovations came about that were all new: atomic bombs and nuclear reactors, transistors and integrated circuits, mass-produced homes, microwave ovens, manned space flight, lasers, xerography, the mouse, PCs, the graphical user interface, the World Wide Web, the Internet search, 3D TV. Significantly, though, many other innovations sprang from earlier developments: radar, cybernetics, television, mass aircraft carriers, ballistic missiles, synthetic rubber, plastics, mass-produced penicillin, and the Green Revolution with high-yield, disease-resistant wheat.

Is mankind, though, moving in decisive style beyond this, the still formidable post-war legacy of innovation?

After the Holocaust and the gulags of the 20th century, the 21st sorely lacks a background culture of optimism about progress. There are few great quests to lighten the load of work: for instance, robots have spread in industry, but still do little in hospital or home. It is labour utilisation, not innovation, that has brought the principal boost to the world economy in recent years.

It's true that there's forward movement in the controlling of IT by voice, face and gesture, in nuclear fusion, cleaner coal, carbon capture and storage, the capture of CO_2 from the air, bio-fuels, batteries and all-electric cars, wind turbines, photovoltaic panels, geothermal energy, hydrology, desalination, early warning systems for bad weather, synthetic biology, stem cell research, neurobiology and much else besides. But there is little to compare with the sweeping grandeur of earlier revolutions.

The emphasis is not on revolutionising production, but rather on finance, home insulation, consumer goods, and consumer services (though something like civilian supersonic transport is out). Innovation has come to mean not step-changes in the making of wealth, but something vaguely akin to the continuous improvement programmes developed in post-war Japanese car factories. There are few new miracle cures, wonder materials or truly rapid transformations of the energy scene. Above all, it is impossible to see even the silhouette of a range of mutually reinforcing innovations, creating new industries across a broad front.

That, though, was the pattern in previous industrial revolutions.

In the second decade of the 21st century, the world badly needs a wave of new industries. Where, for instance, are tomorrow's radically new means of production? The principles around which mankind should go innovating have never been more vital.

References:

[1] Gordon Moore, 'Cramming more components onto integrated circuits', Electronics, Vol 38, No 8, 19 April 1965. The interpretation of complexity and minimum cost is by Jon Stokes, 'Classic.Ars: understanding Moore's law', ars technica, 27 September 2008, on < http://arstechnica.com/hardware/news/2008/09/moore.ars >.

[2] Some see pharmaceutical companies as having 'risen to the challenge' of increased regulation and cost discipline: see Stephen Scypinski, 'Editorial: Speed and Efficiency in Pharmaceutical Development', Journal of Pharmaceutical Innovation, 18 August 2009, on < http://www.springerlink.com/content/c572151612628732/fulltext.pdf >. However for critics, drug firms focus more on 'me-too' innovations than on fundamental ones. In a paradox, just when Big Pharma is attacked for its excessive market power, it has 'a professional sense of gloom' about prospects. See Frank A Sloan and Chee-Ruey Hsieh, Pharmaceutical Innovation: Incentives, Competition, and Cost-benefit, Cambridge University Press, 2007, p10, and Richard A Epstein, Overdose: How Excessive Government Regulation Stifles Pharmaceutical Innovation, Yale University Press, 2006, p7.

[3] Compound interest, like parts of biology and physics, works exponentially; but IT rarely moves as x^t, where x is a constant number bigger than 1, and t, the exponent, represents time elapsed. While Moore's 'law' shows few signs of reaching its limits, in the rest of IT growth tends to be sub-exponential or polynomial. Still more restrictively, around 1980, Metcalfe's law suggested only that the dollar value of a network proceeds as the square of the number of 'compatibly communicating devices'. For a discussion, see Simeon Simeonov, 'Metcalfe's Law: more misunderstood than wrong?', 26 July 2006, on < http://blog.simeonov.com/2006/07/26/metcalfes-law-more-misunderstood-than-wrong/ >.

[4] 'Industrial innovation', noted President Jimmy Carter in a major speech on the subject, 'is an essential, but increasingly overlooked factor in a strong and growing American economy'. See Carter, 'Industrial Innovation Initiatives Remarks Announcing a Program To Encourage Innovation', White House press briefing, 31 October 1979, in John T Woolley and Gerhard Peters, The American Presidency Project [online], Santa Barbara, on < http://www.presidency.ucsb.edu/ws/?pid=31627 >. More than two years earlier, Carter had favoured new, unconventional sources of energy, but only as last of 10 principles: the 'cornerstone' of his response to the energy crisis of 1973-4 was energy conservation. See Carter, 'The President's Proposed Energy Policy', televised speech, 18 April 1977, on < http://www.pbs.org/wgbh/amex/carter/filmmore/ps_energy.html >.

[5] Ray Kurzweil, The Singularity is Near: When Humans Transcend Biology, Viking Adult, 2005, p7. For a pessimist vs an optimist on the rate of technological change, see Jonathan Huebner, 'A possible declining trend for worldwide innovation', Technological Forecasting & Social Change, 72, 2005, on < http://accelerating.org/articles/InnovationHuebner TFSC2005.pdf >, and John Smart, 'Measuring Innovation in an Accelerating World', Acceleration Studies Foundation, no date, on < http://accelerating.org/articles/huebnerinnovation.html >. Two critiques of the view that the speed of change is accelerating are Bob Seidensticker, Future Hype: the Myths of Technology Change, Berrett-Koehler, 2006 and Steven Schnaars, Megamistakes: Forecasting and the Myth of Rapid Technological Change, The Free Press/Collier Macmillan, 1989.

[6] The classic papers from that year are on < http://www.nature.com/nature/dna50/archive.html >.

[7] David Landes, The Unbound Prometheus: Technological Change and Industrial Development in Western Europe from 1750 to the Present, Cambridge University Press, 1969, pp84-85, 87, 90-91, 95, 99, 101-2, 104-5.

[8] Ibid, p235.

[9] See, among others, Alfred Chandler, The Visible Hand: the Managerial Revolution in American Business, Harvard University Press, 1978.

[10] Kevin Maney, The Maverick and His Machine: Thomas Watson, Sr. and the Making of IBM, Wiley, 2003.

[11] James Beniger, The Control Revolution: Technological and Economic Origins of the Information Society, Harvard University Press, 1986.

… # #3
PRINCIPLES NOT MODELS

Innovation cannot prosper without curiosity, serendipity, unpredictable outcomes, inspiring vision, and sheer hard work. But these things are <u>principles</u>, not <u>models</u> of innovation. Market forces may limit innovation, but innovation is too big to be placed on a hockey stick of initial loss followed by profitability, or on a tapering S-curve of market saturation. Nor should the state insist that innovation fits into the straitjackets it lays down.

Nevertheless, in practice one model of innovation dominates today — that it's wrong to focus on pioneering new technologies. [1] 'High-level science and engineering', one savant in America writes, 'are no more important than the ability to use them'.[2] Britain's National Endowment For Science, Technology and the Arts (NESTA), agrees with this. It tells us to emphasise 'business innovation', not the technological sort. [3]

Oh no, innovation cannot, must not begin with laboratories and R&D!

THE SAME OLD TILTS AT THE OLD, LINEAR MODEL

To justify the new, research-lite dogma, everyone attacks the 'linear model' of innovation, which saw it starting from R&D and moving on in a straight line toward commercialisation. NESTA attacks the linear model, hoping that the recession will shift innovation toward 'more open, networked approaches.' [4] But what's new? For Britain's doyen of innovation studies, the late Christopher Freeman, no doctrine on innovation has been 'more frequently attacked and demolished than the so-called linear model'. And he wrote that... in 1996! [5]

Today's innovation theorists are not very innovative. America's John Kao says that firms should network together elements from four international models of innovation. [6] In corporate strategy, too, Gary Hamel tells us to end 'top-down, analytical' methods and instead use models based on biological principles. [7] But why should innovation, a human enterprise, follow models based on IT networks, or on biology? More fundamentally: any theoretical model is merely an artificial device, a metaphor, an analogy, or a rough, formalised or simplified account. So in innovation, any model can, at best, only capture but one way to go. Being a model, the linear account of innovation certainly suffered from all the narrowness of the Cold War epoch, and will not do for the 21st century's more service-based, more global economy. But continued attacks on it now only function as a cipher for a dangerous diversion: underrating the risky, expensive business of R&D.

MODELS AS SUBSTITUTES FOR TECHNOLOGICAL INNOVATION

In place of R&D, the übermodel of innovation today consists of business models. Yet these different ways of reaping revenues from the market — pay as you go, monthly subscription, leasing, lease-purchase, profits through consumables, licensing, franchising and, in the case of Enron, profiting not from energy supply but from derivatives — have a lot to answer for. [8] It's true that innovation cannot be reduced to technology. But to downplay technology in favour of business models is a great mistake.

It's also wrong to talk up an orientation to 'users'. The demand side of innovation is important, but is now widely presented as an <u>alternative</u> to 'technology push'. [9] The latest innovation here is 'design thinking' — an approach, one advocate argues, that 'uses the designer's sensibility and methods to match people's needs with what is technologically feasible'. [10]

Design thinking, design sensibility, design methods — they all sound good. But the UK design community, at least, is, market research suggests, 'apathetic' about boosting its skills. [11] Anyway, matching people's needs to feasible technologies is another cramped model of innovation. Google never started from people's need to search for information. Technologically, its algorithms were feasible, but they were also new, and specially developed.

In fact, taking one's lead from users exemplifies a wider trend. For much of the noughties, Harvard's Henry Chesbrough has said that that firms should <u>rely on others</u> to innovate for them. Innovation must change from closed to open, basing itself on a 'landscape of abundant knowledge' lying not just with customers, but also with other companies, suppliers, universities, national laboratories, industrial consortia, and start-up firms. [12]

Who, though, would today want to boast of running a <u>closed</u> innovation system? Openness sounds hip, but in outsourcing innovation, it abdicates each organisation's responsibility to lead and perform innovation itself. Now that we have found out about Bernie Madoff, but still don't know where the banks' toxic assets are, it's clear that we <u>don't</u> live in a landscape of abundant knowledge. In assuming what cannot be assumed, open models of innovation are complacent, self-serving, and a cop-out.

Innovation is none of these things. It is not just a combination of what has gone before, as some maintain. [13]

Innovation is based on new knowledge, or it is nothing.

References:

[1] An important exception to this rule is Clayton Christensen. See his <u>The Innovator's Dilemma: When New Technologies Cause Great Firms to Fail</u>, Harvard Business Press, 1997, and with Michael E Raynor, his <u>The Innovator's Solution: Creating and Sustaining Successful Growth</u>, Harvard Business Press, 2003.

[2] Amar Bhidé, 'Where innovation creates value', <u>The McKinsey Quarterly</u>, February 2009. For more, see Bhidé, <u>The Venturesome Economy: How Innovation Sustains Prosperity in a More Connected World</u>, Princeton University Press, 2008.

[3] Charles Leadbeater and James Meadway, Attacking the Recession: How Innovation can Fight the Downturn, NESTA Discussion Paper, December 2008, p12.

[4] Ibid, p11.

[5] Chris Freeman, 'The greening of technology and models of innovation', Technological Forecasting and Social Change, No 53, 1996, pp27-39.

[6] John Kao, 'Tapping the world's innovation hotspots', Harvard Business Review, March 2009.

[7] Gary Hamel, 'Moon shots for management', Harvard Business Review, February 2009.

[8] For more on business models, see James Woudhuysen and Joe Kaplinsky, Energise! A Future for Energy Innovation, Beautiful Books, 2009, Chapter 7.

[9] Useful, but tending to this view are Donald Norman, The Psychology of Everyday Things, Basic Books, 1988; John Seely Brown and others, Storytelling in Organizations: Why Storytelling Is Transforming 21st Century Organizations and Management, Butterworth-Heinemann, 2004, and Eric Von Hippel, Democratizing Innovation, MIT Press, 2005.

[10] Tim Brown, 'Design thinking', Harvard Business Review, June 2008, p86. For more, see Brown, Change by Design: How Design Thinking Transforms Organizations and Inspires Innovation, HarperBusiness, 2009.

[11] Angus Montgomery, 'Design community "slow to boost its skills"', Design Week, 24 February 2009, on < http://www.designweek.co.uk/news/design-community-'slow-to-boost-its-skills'/1141384.article > (subscription required).

[12] Henry Chesbrough, Open Innovation: the New Imperative for Creating and Profiting from Technology, Harvard Business School Press, 2003, and Open Business Models: How to Thrive in the New Innovation Landscape, Harvard Business School Press, 2006.

[13] See for example Frans Johansson, The Medici Effect: What Elephants and Epidemics Can Teach Us About Innovation, Harvard Business School Press, 2004; Scott Berkun, The Myths of Innovation, O'Reilly UK, 2007; Charles Leadbeater, 'Shanghai: The Innovative City', Speech to Mayor of Shanghai's International Business Leaders Advisory Council, 5 November 2009, on < http://www.charlesleadbeater.net/archive/shanghai-iblac-speech.aspx >.

#4
IN PRAISE OF 'USELESS' RESEARCH

In our cynical, short-attention-span age, it has become imperative to rally to the defence of pure, basic, long-term research. R&D isn't just D. Without aggressive R, there will be no major, new or surprising industries.

Governments and business have steadily backed off from investing in pure research. A key moment, perhaps, came in 1993, when the US Congress cancelled plans for a Superconducting Super Collider facility in Texas.

Today, even a research project like Europe's Large Hadron Collider feels called upon to say that one of its byproducts may be new science, 'that can be applied almost immediately'. [1]

Once research is justified like this, however, it loses its reason for being. As Einstein is reputed to have said, 'If we knew what we were doing, it wouldn't be called research.'

FROM PROGRESS TO EXPEDIENCY

If ever there was a golden age of scientific endeavour, in which discovery was felt to have its own merits, that age was the Enlightenment of the 17th and especially the 18th centuries. Science was seen as critical to progress. But in the 20th century, it was embraced for more pragmatic reasons, and, not least, in the pursuit of military power.

In 2010, pure research is widely regarded as a bit of a luxury. Having lost faith in progress and the future, society is besieged by fear of the unknown. In a culture that reveres the predictable, the tangible and the knowable, only the short-term musters interest.

The phrase 'blue skies' research is today said with a sneer. Yet research cannot be conceived of in narrow, instrumentalist terms, as a means of getting pre-cast 'impacts' for UK PLC. In December 2009, UK chancellor Alastair Darling added £200m to a modest (£750m) Strategic Investment Fund for next-generation industries. Announcing that fund earlier, science and industry minister Lord Drayson said he wanted it devoted to those sectors in which Britain had a clear competitive advantage, in which growth opportunities to 2029 were significant, and in which Britain was likely to be the No 1 or No 2 in the world. [2] However, as an excellent and widely signed petition to No 10 Downing Street observed, it's wrong to direct funds to projects whose outcomes are specified in advance. [3]

RETRIEVING THE ARGUMENTS FOR BASIC RESEARCH

It's true that the giant companies that used to do a lot of pure research — for example, Bell, or Xerox — rarely benefited from it. But it's also true that the firms that have ridden to success on the back of the efforts of others have rarely reinvested profits to finance new rounds of research. Indeed, pure research is so scarce, people have forgotten what it's for. As a result, some things need restating.

Research leads to the <u>production</u> of new knowledge. That's different from the <u>transfer</u> of <u>existing</u> knowledge. The practice humanity needs is <u>better than</u> existing 'best practice'.

The fundamental unpredictability of research nourishes new experimental methods, turns up new problems, and opens up fresh avenues of enquiry. As a result, research creates not simply incremental advance, but, in many cases, whole new industries.

Each proposal for research proposals needs assessing in its own terms. Is it unique, daring, insightful, comprehensive, unprejudiced, elegant in its approach, tough to execute but doable at a stretch? Does it push beyond the familiar and challenge orthodoxies in an exciting way?

What may be thought 'useless' research today may, in two or more decades' time, become profoundly useful. One just doesn't know.

All one knows is that research is nothing without unremitting curiosity and tenacious application.

References:

[1] 'Who benefits?', LHC UK, on < http://www.lhc.ac.uk/about-the-lhc/who-benefits.html >.

[2] Drayson, 'Innovation in recession and recovery', Speech to Scientific-Economic Research Union conference, Berlin, 6 May 2009, on < http://www.dius.gov.uk/news_and_speeches/speeches/lord_drayson/innovation_recession >.

[3] Petition asking the Prime Minister to promote discovery and innovation in UK science, Number 10.gov.uk, 3 October 2009, on < http://petitions.number10.gov.uk/honest-discovery >. For Gordon Brown's typically evasive and ambiguous reply, see 'Honest-discovery – epetition response [sic]', Number 10.gov.uk, 29 October 2009, on < http://www.number10.gov.uk/Page21111 >.

#5 INNOVATION IS HARD WORK

It offends contemporary sensibilities to say so, but what Thomas Edison famously said of genius — that it is one per cent inspiration and 99 per cent perspiration — remains largely true of innovation.

Given that mankind's imaginings are so often, nowadays, confined to lurid scenes of future chaos, the power and utility of scientific, technological and other kinds of inspiration should never be underestimated. But nor does innovation grow on trees. Serendipity is important in science, but as Louis Pasteur said, `In the field of observation, chance favours only the prepared mind'. [1] To establish the structure of a molecule can come to someone in a dream, but to dream that special dream one must spend years thinking about and experimenting with chemistry — and to do something useful with that molecule, still more years.

Society's elites are not scrupulous enough in preparing for the Next Big Thing. They are open to someone else's innovation, or to the outsourcing of innovation, but would rather not do it themselves. Elites don't much believe in building yet another prototype or demonstration. They are deliciously interdisciplinary in outlook, of course; but real, in-depth specialisation in one discipline has become conspicuous by its absence.

IN INNOVATION, THERE'S NO SUCH THING AS A FREE LUNCH

Today's myriad different kinds of networks distribute innovations, but do not by themselves create them. However fast they operate, new media are no substitute for content-rich innovation. Innovatory firms may cluster together in particular geographical regions, cities and localities; yet even in Silicon Valley, where once there was a passion for telling all, people don't any more exchange much serious intellectual property in the pub.

IP is so hard to come by, it's felt too valuable for that.

Much — though not all — of science today is freely exchanged, and open access to scientific journals is growing. But in the commercial world of intellectual property the accent is often more on the property than on the intellectual. The work of patent and copyright lawyers is more valued than the work of innovators, even if it is probably innovators who have to work harder.

In software, open source has much to recommend it. In astronomy, the use of thousands of PCs in parallel shows some of the merits of 'crowd-sourcing'. But in both of these cases, large numbers of people have to work large numbers of hours to make a difference. Yes, in innovation there's no such thing as a free lunch.

INNOVATION IS AN UPHILL STRUGGLE

There is no need to revive the moralism of the Protestant work ethic. Too much work on innovation lacks focus, and careful, collective discussion:

today's innovation processes often make extravagant use of people's time. But there is a need to stop the pretence that innovation can be reduced simply to creativity. There is also a need to destroy the myth that creativity is simply the playful combination of existing elements. As we have already noted, innovation cannot consist of combination; anyway, combining the old takes a lot of hard work.

It is time that students, in particular, learned that innovation involves meeting setbacks, blind alleys, frustrations, polemics, long periods of patient perplexity, and the occasional humiliation in front of one's peers.

Innovation means making something new. Brand extensions, line extensions and 'new, improved' don't qualify for the title. Innovation is not done in a day. It is a struggle uphill, and there is plenty that is noble in that.

References:

[1] Pasteur, Lecture at the University of Lille, 7 December 1854.

#6
FOR SUCCESS, EXPECT LOTS OF FAILURES

Today, innovation often feels called upon to apologise for the drain on resources it represents, and for the dangers it may bring. No wonder it just as often portrays itself as broadly <u>predictable</u>. [1] To gain support, it can pretend to be a smooth process, uninterrupted by false turns, intractable difficulties, personal clashes, or budgetary mishaps.

In fact, though, a single serious innovation is invariably preceded by multiple failures. There is no need to be sentimental about failure being a badge of honour in Silicon Valley, or to be fascinated by failure. [2] Success remains the objective worth striving for. Yet as America's Henry Petroski has written, the lessons learned from disasters 'can do more to advance engineering knowledge than all the successful machines and structures in the world'. [3] Over 1990-2009, its production years, even a $5 billion failed enterprise like General Motors' Saturn division gave the car industry many lessons on what to do and what not to do in future. [4]

In a scientific experiment, a negative result can be even more instructive than a positive one. In the same way prototypes, an indispensable stage in innovation, would not be prototypes if most did not fail.

To deliver a bright future, innovation requires bold experiments — and, sometimes, big failures. This is not a matter of recommending, as Gordon Brown used to do, that the UK ape the liberal provisions of American law in relation to business bankruptcies. It is, rather, about recognising that the failure-laden process of scientific and technological innovation has the merit of converting major uncertainties into risks — risks that are quantifiable and frequently modest. More often than not, failure is a price worth paying for success.

Take the example of nuclear fusion. For many years, the world has failed to demonstrate that this technique can generate proper quantities of electricity. Yet that record of failure doesn't mean that commercial nuclear fusion will always remain 30 years away. Too many make such a cynical, one-sided judgement. Much has been learned.

FAILURE CANNOT BE AVOIDED

Since the credit crunch, fears that starting a new business will end in failure have risen in economies stretching from Argentina to Finland. [5] In America, the proportion of adults fearing that their creation of a new business could end in failure is 28 per cent. In Britain, the figure is 38 per cent — and elsewhere, the figures are much worse (Japan 44, Italy 48, Germany 49, Spain 52, France 53). [6]

To fear failure at the modest scale of the individual entrepreneur is only a symptom of what, for society, is a much wider problem. If teachers cannot allow students to encounter and learn how to recover from setbacks, those students will not look positively on experiment and action. If, among organisations, there is fear that the costs, schedules and payoffs of innovation are too tough to meet, then habit will return to using only what has gone before. Yet in innovation as in life itself, failure cannot be avoided.

In today's economic adversity, many incline to hold back from innovation, preferring to pause, retrench, and wait until the storm blows over. They forget that this storm was itself caused not by failed innovations, but by the failure to make enough serious and connected innovations across a broad front, and certainly outside the financial sector.

Failed innovations are anyway worth preserving. Human effort went into these failures; indeed, whole careers were bound up with them. Nevertheless, insights were gained. In the future, too, separate innovations may help set this set of poor results, or that project stupidly terminated, in a brighter context.

A failure in innovation can rule out a line of enquiry, can challenge assumptions, or can prove the spur to the development of a simpler device.

In innovation, every failure is a success of sorts.

References:

[1] Clayton Christensen and Michael Raynor make the mistake of thinking that innovation can be predictable. See The Innovator's Solution, op cit.

[2] For the sentimentality about Silicon Valley, see for example Tom Peters, The Circle of Innovation: You Can't Shrink Your Way To Greatness, Vintage, 1999, pp85, 86. For the fascination with failure now laid at the door of Generation Y, see Associated Press, 'Failure 101: A class students could use', msnbc, 5 November 2009, on < http://www.msnbc.msn.com/id/33673507 >.

[3] Henry Petroski, To Engineer is Human: the Role of Failure in Successful Design, Macmillan, 1985, page x.

[4] 'Saturn: a wealth of lessons from failure', Knowledge@Wharton.com, 28 October 2009, on < http://knowledge.wharton.upenn.edu/article.cfm?articleid=2366 >.

[5] Niels Bosma and others, Global Entrepreneurship Monitor 2008 Executive Report, 2008, Figure 4, page 17, on < http://www.gemconsortium.org/download.asp?fid=849 >.

[6] Ibid, Table 1, p16.

#7 REGARD CHANCE AND SURPRISE AS ALLIES

In 1928, while on holiday, the Scots biologist and pharmacologist Alexander Fleming accidentally left a number of cultures of staphylococcus bacteria uncovered. He returned to find the growth of bacteria in one dish inhibited by a growing blue-green fungus, <u>Penicillium notatum</u>. Penicillin, which Fleming named after filtering it off from a hot solution of the fungus, was later found to dispose of several of the world's major diseases.

From the microwave oven through the Post-it note and on to the Viagra pill, serendipity — a random turn of events that proves fortuitous — has played a major role in the process of innovation. [1] Yet if 21st century managers always say they're ready for 'out of the box' thinking, in practice many bridle at the idea of an innovation project moving sideways. Why should chance, tangential discoveries absorb researchers in the unexpected, the unfamiliar, the difficult, and the costly?

Innovation processes can lead many organisations down paths they would rather not go. But that is precisely what is valuable about them. Their logic is not the logic of the market. Innovation needs planning; but one cannot really plan for its intrinsically serendipitous character.

AS HUMAN ENDEAVOURS, INNOVATION AND TECHNOLOGY WILL SURPRISE

Like surprises in the process of innovation, the history of 'finished' technological products and systems is the history of transformations for the most part unforeseen. As the Internet bears witness, technologies conceived for one use have acquired other, unexpected uses over time.

Why do typical processes of innovation share with the social evolution of technology the capacity to bring about pleasant surprises? Because the fate of both depends on a surprising species: humanity. It's real men and women that not only originate innovations, but also chance upon them, and continuously adapt them to new ends.

To discover the uses of things is the work of history-making human beings. The ocean, once seen as a barrier, in time became a means for human development and exploration.

It is not the atomic nucleus that makes for nuclear war, but the plans of men. It is not the Internet that creates democracy, but political action. It is not newly engineered houses that create community, but the people who live in them. It is social circumstances, not the functionalities within a technology, which dictate how, in different times and places, it will be adopted, rejected, used or abused. Any other view of innovation would fall into technological determinism, in which technology is held to have a relentless logic not subject to the preferences of society.

Luckily enough, however, innovation and technology always contain the possibility of happy accidents, not just unhappy ones.

LET'S HEAR IT FOR UNANTICIPATED NEEDS

Yes, necessity is the mother of invention. But inventions themselves call forth new needs. [2] Nobody needed the carwash before the car.

#7: REGARD CHANCE AND SURPRISE AS ALLIES

Nobody needed uranium much before atomic weapons and atomic power were established.

In innovation, the concept of the unexpected deserves continued acclaim, for that shows confidence in human ingenuity. Human beings can solve problems thrown at them, can take advantage of fresh insights, and can usefully invent new problems to solve. Most of the time, that will tend to make scientific and technical surprises a source of delight, not despondency.

Will the generation of new and unanticipated needs, through technology, lead to further problems? Perhaps. But many tricky problems, old and new, must be solved if society is to go beyond the post-war legacy of innovation.

References:

[1] In 1945, radar researcher Percy Spencer noticed that his equipment had melted a bar of chocolate he had on him; after that he and his employer, Raytheon, patented and built microwave ovens. In 1968 3M scientist Dr Spencer Silver made a glue of clear, sparkly spheres rather than film: it could be used again and again, but wasn't very sticky. Only when Silver's colleague, Art Fry, found himself repeatedly losing the bookmark in his church hymnbook did it occur to 3M to develop an application for that glue as repositionable pieces of paper. Today, more than 600 Post-it products are sold in more than 100 countries. See 3M, 'Post-it Note History', on < http://www.3m.com/us/office/postit/pastpresent/history.html >.

In 1996 pharmaceutical chemists at Pfizer developed a new compound in the hope of treating high blood pressure and cases of reduced blood supply to the heart. Clinical trials at Swansea showed few benefits around angina, but an unexpected side effect: penile erections. By 2008 sales of Viagra had topped $1.9 billion — see Pfizer, entry for Viagra in 'Key medicines and their performance', Doing Things Differently: Annual Review 2008, on < http://www.pfizer.com/investors/financial_reports/annual_reports/key_medicines.jsp >.

[2] See David E Nye, Technology Matters: Questions to Live With, The MIT Press, 2006, p2.

#8
TAKE RISKS

In 2005, China's engineers and scientists completed a new railway. Splicing through mountains five kilometres high and underground rock formations where the temperatures run at -30°C, the new line stretches from Golmud in the province of Qinghai to Lhasa, the capital of Tibet. No fewer than 1,142 km long, it was finished three years ahead of schedule. [1]

The railway is a triumph not just of engineering, but also of conscious risk-taking. Barriers thought very hard to overcome were proved surmountable.

That sequence of events, in which risks are confronted, is a relative rarity these days.

For some years before the credit crunch, organisations made the management of risk into a fearful obsession. [2] Right now, though, however, the consultants Booz, though in favour of innovation, nevertheless want firms to develop a 'risk appetite' in the sense of 'a company-wide statement of the amount of risk that is desirable in day-to-day affairs'. [3] An expert in supply chains says that, given globalisation, just-in-time scheduling, the Internet, the offshoring and outsourcing of labour, the outsourcing of production and manufacturing, and the virtualisation of workplaces or their consolidation it into 'single points of failure', then risk consciousness needs to be 'pervasive' among all the stakeholders of each organisation's value chains. [4]

Around innovation, however, there is already far too much risk consciousness. For in innovation, rules and routine often need to be overturned. Innovation is an inherently risky business. Yet it is at the same time often the best way to deal with risks.

INNOVATION IS RISKY. GET OVER IT

Nowadays, men and women are supposed everywhere to be 'at risk', because everywhere they stand guilty of past misdeeds with nature. In the same way society's image of the innovator has moved from heroic boffin (Bletchley Park and Alan Turing in the Second World War), through likable eccentric (Emmett 'Doc' Brown in Robert Zemeckis' Back to the Future, 1985), to crazed psycho (Dr Gerard 'supergun' Bull, 1928-90, or Dr Craig Venter today).

In 1982, the intrepid Australian physician Barry James Marshall drank a billion Helicobacter pylori to prove the bacterial origins of ulcers. Along with his colleague J Robin Warren, Marshall won the 2005 Nobel Prize for Physiology or Medicine. [5] Yet few outside the world of medicine celebrate the example Marshall set. [6] Instead, something else has happened.

Elites have come to hold nature as vengeful and in possession of autonomous and highly dangerous risks. Nature is secretly apprehended as thoughtful. By contrast, human beings, and with them innovators, are loudly held to be unthinking, careless, arrogant, power-mad. Yet this turns the world on its head. It presents mankind as in a kind of permanent bipolar disorder — as afflicted by both evil and vulnerability.

It reverses the idea of the innovator acting, like Barry Marshall, on the world. Instead, the 'innovator' is now the subject to be acted upon, constrained, placed under legal control.

Talking up the inevitable risks of innovation can only paralyse even the planning of innovation, to say nothing of its execution. Yet innovation has always been risky. Its arc of development cannot be forecast beforehand.

It is time to overturn the Precautionary Principle, upheld at the United Nations Rio Summit of 1992 and adopted by the European Commission in 2000. Defenders of the Principle always present it as something which, when applied, demands action and innovation. But by dramatising ill-defined uncertainties and refusing to make a balanced calibration of risks, the Precautionary Principle renders the very idea of innovation a suspect one. The Principle is about stopping human beings doing anything thought uncertain, not about starting new and risky innovations.

CONSCIOUS INNOVATION IS THE BEST WAY TO DEAL WITH RISKS

Human consciousness is of use, anyway, not just in the registration of risks, but also, and much more, in the application and extension of accumulated knowledge through experiment. Innovation, though it includes the action of chance, is a thoughtful act based upon wisdom built up over time. At least in principle, therefore, innovation betokens a growing ability to mitigate risks.

In his influential Risk Society (1986), Ulrich Beck, the great magnifier of risk, represented innovation as just the opposite of this.

For Beck innovation is not slowing down, as this Manifesto, says, but exists, rather, in an epoch in which it is 'set free'. There are 'waves of large-scale technological innovation with as yet unknown future hazards'. Medical progress is institutionalised without the lay public's consent, for 'medicine possesses a free pass for the implementation and testing of its "innovations"'. [7]

Altogether, Beck held innovation as a source of risk, as running amok. More recently, he has discovered that, with climate change, 'the multibillion-Euro EU budget can give a boost to innovations, from alternative energy sources through to energy-efficient technologies' — even if, more generally, 'innovations are always good for companies, only rarely for human beings'. [8]

In fact, in the wake of Copenhagen, the EU will provide 'fast-start funding' around climate change to the tune of just €7.2 billion over the years 2010-12. [9] The US and Australian governments, and the EU, likewise committed a total of just $4 billion to back 13 demonstration projects in Carbon Capture and Storage. [10] There are plans for larger EU-side schemes in renewable energy; but these are plans only. [11]

There is no need to overstate the risk of climate disaster. But it would be hard to enthuse about the West's commitment to innovation around climate change, the key target of government policy nowadays.

The situation is the opposite of what Beck says. We risk difficulties not because of too much innovation, but because of too little.

References:

[1] Jonathan Watts, 'The railway across the roof of the world', The Guardian, 20 December 2005, on < http://www.guardian.co.uk/world/2005/sep/20/china.jonathanwatts >.

[2] To give but one example: when George Bush launched the President's Management Agenda in 2002, it noted that, according to the General Accounting Office (GAO) 'high-risk' list, the number of areas in US federal government most vulnerable to fraud, waste, and abuse had in 10 years risen from eight to 22. See Executive Office Of The President Office Of Management And Budget, The President's Management Agenda, Fiscal Year 2002, on < http://www.whitehouse.gov/omb/budget/fy2002/mgmt.pdf >.

[3] Alan Gemes and Peter T Golder, 'What Is Your Risk Appetite?', strategy+business, 30 November 2009, on < http://www.strategy-business.com/article/00010?pg=all >.

[4] Gary S Lynch, At Your Own Risk: How the Risk-Conscious Culture Meets the Challenge of Business Change, Wiley 2008, p5 and Chapter 2.

[5] Martin B Van Der Weyden and others, 'The 2005 Nobel Prize in Physiology or Medicine', The Medical Journal of Australia, Vol 183 No 11/12, on < http://www.mja.com.au/public/issues/183_11_051205/van11000_fm.html#0_i1091639 >.

[6] In fact Marshall stands in a long medical tradition. See Lawrence K Altman, Who Goes First? The Story of Self-Experimentation in Medicine (1986), University of California Press, 1998.

[7] Ulrich Beck, Risk Society: Towards a New Modernity (1986), Sage, 1992, pp11, 185, 206, 207.

[8] Ulrich Beck, World at Risk, Polity, 2009, pp62, 213.

[9] European Council, Conclusions – 10/11 December 2009, EUCO 6/09, 11 December 2009, p13, on < http://www.consilium.europa.eu/uedocs/cms_data/docs/pressdata/en/ec/111877.pdf >.

[10] Global CCS Institute, 'Governments commit USD$4bn to global Carbon Capture and Storage (CCS) projects', press release, 16 December 2009, on < http://www.globalccsinstitute.com/downloads/media-releases/MR_Govts-commit-USD$4bn-to-global-CCS-projects.pdf >.

[11] Alok Jha, 'Sun, wind and wave-powered: Europe unites to build renewable energy "supergrid"', Guardian.co.uk, 3 January 2010, on < http://www.guardian.co.uk/environment/2010/jan/03/european-unites-renewable-energy-supergrid >.

#9 INNOVATION DEMANDS LEADERSHIP

The more the cult of celebrity extends into everyday life, it seems, the more distaste grows for celebrity leaders of innovation.

British engineer Isambard Kingdom Brunel, New York city planner Robert Moses, Intel chip designer Robert Noyce, Russian space programme chief Sergei Korolev, Japan's Soichiro Honda: in innovation, as in life, strong leaders are essential. Yet for some years the trend in general management theory has been away from the charismatic leader and toward the servant leader or the self-confessedly incomplete one. [1] Today, the leader is vulnerable or he is nothing.

Books eulogise successful Americans and others for their past failures. [2] They explore the merits, to innovation, not of personal leaders, but of <u>teams</u> as a means of 'distributed' leadership. [3] It's said that to 're-imagine' innovation with workforces now both virtual and global, what's needed is the <u>ambassadorial</u> leader who is sensitive to culture and context, and who shares leadership. [4] More broadly, feeling favours leadership communities, rather than great leaders. [5]

That's more than enough New Age thinking on leadership. Some hold that happiness and managing your energy levels are two of the five dimensions of leadership. [6] Britain's National Health Service Institute for Innovation and Improvement, no less, puts at the core of leadership not the setting of directions or the delivery of service, but self-belief, self-awareness, self-management, a drive for personal improvement, and personal integrity — in short, our old friends 'me, me, me'. [7]

In fact leadership in innovation should not and cannot be diffused away from a few individual leaders. At the same time, leadership is bigger than the Self. Distinct and distinctive leaders are required not only to get innovation moving, but also to set aspirations, create goals that people can believe in, and take responsibility for failures. Innovation leaders must have both breadth and depth of technical knowledge. But they must also be able to inspire. Innovation is a human process; because it includes failure and chance, it must be led by men and women who can take people from their 'comfort zones' into a different place altogether.

RESTATING THE CASE FOR LEADERS

In 2010 leadership, like innovation, is in doubt. Leaders are blamed for economic failure, for political corruption, or for not paying heed to signs of trouble. Of course, they have grown specially fallible to the degree that they have become answerable only to themselves. Faith in them has also dwindled, however, because they so rarely stand for anything beyond managing the status quo.

What a pity, then, it is to learn, from an intelligent handbook on the leadership of innovation, that 'the age of the autocratic boss, the one-man show, is over' and that 'innovation should always be evolutionary rather than revolutionary'. [8] But did prima donnas really always dominate 20th century innovation — or is that another straw man? And doesn't the leadership of innovation mean guiding others to make both evolutionary and revolutionary advance?

To restate the case for innovation means to restate the case for all-round leadership. Both are at risk in an atmosphere that one-sidedly promotes partnership, participation and networking — in a word, collaboration. [9] All of these things have their place, and we are all for international collaboration in R&D. But right now the personal ability to create new knowledge, and to take an innovation problem or project by the scruff of the neck and make it happen, is an item in much shorter supply than windy phrases about the ability to absorb global innovations — to 'access, absorb, spread and apply ideas and concepts generated elsewhere'. [10]

Leadership, like innovation, is now something you network. But including everyone in an 'innovation culture' can all too easily mean abdicating responsibility.

THE INNOVATOR AS HERO

In 2007, the consultants McKinsey surveyed more than 700 of the world's senior vice presidents and more than 700 of its lower-level executives, too. About a third of the middle and lower layers said they managed innovation on an ad hoc basis when necessary. Another third managed innovation as part of the senior-leadership team's agenda. But that was largely it. To their credit, 600 global business executives, managers, and professionals also surveyed by McKinsey admitted that paying lip service to innovation but doing nothing about it was the most common way they inhibited it. [11]

McKinsey had many recommendations. Perhaps the most familiar was: set performance metrics for innovation — metrics both financial and, to catch today's climate, also behavioural. [12] Yet the key McKinsey metric seems to be that, to 'upgrade' R&D in a downturn, 'the most vigilant product developers could terminate one-quarter to one-third of their projects, liberating resources for redeployment'. [13]

In fact what innovation needs now, if it is to be game-changing, unique and unexpected, is leaders with resolve, not managers with finely balanced scalpels.

Innovation demands not further empathy, trust or Key Performance Indicators, but vision, commitment, brains and, yes, a little personal heroism too.

References:

[1] Robert K Greenleaf, Servant Leadership, Paulist Press, 1983; Deborah Ancona and others, 'In praise of the incomplete leader', Harvard Business Review, February 2007, on < http://www.fapsconline.org/hmm/leading_and_motivating.zip/resources/R0702E.pdf >.

[2] See Warren G Bennis and Robert J Thomas, Geeks and Geezers: How Era, Values, and Defining Moments Shape Leaders, Harvard Business School Press, 2002. In a more popular genre, see Steve Young, Great Failures Of The Extremely Successful: Mistakes, Adversity, Failure And Other Stepping Stones To Success, Tallfellow Press, 2002; John A Sarkett, Extraordinary Comebacks, Sourcebooks, 2007, and Joey Green, Famous Failures: Hundreds Of Hot Shots Who Got Rejected, Flunked Out, Worked Lousy Jobs, Goofed Up, Or Did Time In Jail Before Achieving Phenomenal Success, Lunatic Press, 2007.

[3] See for example Deborah Ancona and Henrik Bresman, X-teams: How to Build Teams That Lead, Innovate and Succeed, Harvard Business School Press, 2007.

[4] Karen Sobel Lojeski and Richard R Reilly, Uniting the Virtual Workforce: Transforming Leadership and Innovation in the Globally Integrated Enterprise, Wiley, 2008, pp131, 132 and Chapter 7.

[5] Gianpiero Petriglieri, Affiliate Professor of Organisational Behaviour at INSEAD, quoted in Shellie Karabell, 'Leadership today: less charisma, more consensus', INSEAD Knowledge, 18 December 2009, on < http://knowledge.insead.edu/leadership-insead-initiative.cfm?vid=362 >.

[6] Joanna Barsh and others, 'Five dimensions of leadership', McKinsey Quarterly, 2008, Issue 4.

[7] NHS Institute for Innovation and Improvement, 'NHS leadership qualities framework', on < http://www.nhsleadershipqualities.nhs.uk/portals/0/the_framework.pdf >.

[8] John Adair, Leadership for Innovation: How to Organize Team Creativity and Harvest Ideas, Kogan Page, 2007, pp65, 122.

[9] See for example Michael M Beyerlein and others, Innovation Through Collaboration, Advances in Interdisciplinary Studies of Work Teams Volume 12, JAI Press, 2006.

[10] NESTA, Absorbing Global Innovations: Access, Anchor, Diffuse, Policy briefing, October 2008, on < http://www.nesta.org.uk/library/documents/Policy%20Brief%20-%20Absorbing%20Global%20Innovations%20v4.pdf >.

[11] Joanna Barsh and others, 'Leadership and innovation', McKinsey Quarterly, January 2008.

[12] Ibid.

[13] Christie W Barrett and others, 'Upgrading R&D in a downturn', McKinsey Quarterly, February 2009.

#10 INNOVATION IS EVERYBODY'S RESPONSIBILITY

Innovation is not just for private firms, large and small. In different ways, it is also for nations, public sector organisations, and for other, 'third sector' bodies.

If innovation is for every substantial body in society, it is not for everyone, sadly enough. After all, science and technology require specialisation, so that not every person can be an innovator.

Anyway, innovation is, as we have said, bigger than science and technology alone. It encompasses changes in organisation. It can include changes in design.

THE 'WHO' OF INNOVATION

It might appear obvious that innovation is a task for national economies, but critics of the 'national innovation systems' approach to innovation now prefer to present innovation in the terms of Manuel Castells — as a global flow, something easily dipped into. According to the London think tank Demos,

'It may be that innovation is becoming global first and supported by national innovation systems second....

'National competition might not have the relevance it once had. We are entering an age of global interdependence of innovation.' [1]

Well, yes and no. Lawyers and intelligence services exist to prevent the flow of particular kinds of science, and quite a lot of technology, around the world.

Of course, Demos feels that 'a national pride in innovation is admirable'. [2] We don't agree — but it is too early to conclude that the nation state has been superceded as a force for innovation.

One of the reasons for this is the size of the public sector, even in the US. There, innovation can be as weak, if not weaker, than it is in the private sector. In Britain, the now-defunct Department of Industry, Universities and Skills (DIUS) made much of the fact that it committed a princely £525,000 in 2008/9 to the development of innovation in the UK public sector. [3] Perhaps that gives some hint of why, over 1997 to 2007, the productivity of UK public services fell by 3.4 per cent, an annual average of 0.3 per cent. [4]

Innovation is, finally, a matter for voluntary organisations. Even a text which maintains that US non-profit organisations are innovative, that foundations are 'founts' of innovation, and that fundraising in the past couple of years has seen a lot of innovation, is forced to concede that the potential 'to meet the needs of the underclass' is matched by 'the formidable challenges of delivering'. [5]

INNOVATION AS NEW ORGANISATION

With technological innovations in process come changes in organisation. And as Alfred Sloan of General Motors showed in the 1920s, with his annual model change and his divisionalisation of GM, changes in organisation can go ahead even in the absence of radical new technologies. [6] Yet for all the ceaseless changes in Britain's public sector bureaucracy over the past 10 years, real progress in organisation, with or without technology, has been largely absent.

In the public sector, innovation is now supposed to be about co-production, or delivering public services 'in an equal and reciprocal relationship between professionals, people using services, their families and their neighbours'. [7] In cultural institutions, which often rely on public funds, the same recipe obtains: what is called for is 'a focus away from product-centric towards experience-centric innovation' — that is, innovation in which value is created through 'co-created experiences in which the operator (eg a museum), the visitor and the community of visitors take part'. [8]

Here organisational innovations to achieve increased efficiency are irrelevant, because efficiency 'isn't effective'. [9] Well: it is indeed an ABC of management that efficiency (doing things right) is not the same as effectiveness (doing the right things). But when it is learned that radical innovation in the public sector means 'reducing demand for expensive critical services', [10] perhaps a few old-fashioned efficiencies, based on new ways of organising, would not be such a bad idea after all.

THE ROLE OF DESIGN AND BRANDING

Design and even clear branding, as a means of signposting the world, have their place in innovation. It's true that an innovatory chair, for example, can be based purely on an ingenious new design, and not on new materials or production techniques. It's also true that the provision of a new railway service need not necessarily rely on new technology — and that information design will be needed as part of the package.

The role of design and branding, however, is not to engage in special pleading that would make them a substitute for new technology. Designers and brandsmiths should stop wringing their hands about involving users and saving the planet, and instead start taking seriously their role as the humanising handmaidens of technological innovation.

References:

[1] Kirsten Bound and others, The New Geography of Innovation: India, Finland, Science and Technology, Sitra Reports 71, 2006, p15, on < http://www.sitra.fi/julkaisut/raportti71.pdf >.

[2] Ibid.

[3] DIUS, Annual Innovation Report 2008, December 2008, p49, on < http://www.dius.gov.uk/innovation/innovation_nation/~/media/publications/2/21390%20AIR%20Report%20AW%20Complete >.

[4] Office for National Statistics, Total Public Service Output and Productivity, 9 June 2009, as corrected on 14 August 2009, on < http://www.statistics.gov.uk/articles/nojournal/TotalPublicServiceFinalv5.pdf >.

[5] Steven H Goldberg, Billions of Drops in Millions of Buckets: Why Philanthropy Doesn't Advance Social Progress, Wiley, 2009, pages xxviii, 99, 103.

[6] See Alfred Sloan, My Years with General Motors (1963).

[7] David Boyle and Michael Harris, The Challenge of Co-Production, NESTA and the New Economics Foundation, December 2009, p11, on < http://www.nesta.org.uk/library/documents/Co-production-report.pdf >.

[8] Hasan Bakhshi and David Throsby, Innovation in Arts and Cultural Organisations, NESTA interim research report, December 2009, on < http://www.nesta.org.uk/library/documents/Innovation-in-arts-and-cultural-interim.pdf >.

[9] Boyle and Harris, op cit, p9.

[10] Ibid.

# 11
TRUST THE PEOPLE, NOT REGULATION

The Regulators do not trust the people. Yet the people do not trust the Regulators. Partisans of innovation need to take the right side in this dispute. It's time for them to state unequivocally that further state laws and regulations around innovation are in general likely to circumscribe it and slow it down, not enhance it. You don't have to be a believer in free market forces to agree with that.

Since the credit crunch, the world's governments have failed to innovate in economic analysis. Instead, they have disinterred the patrician economics and statist politics of John Maynard Keynes. Meanwhile free markets, the same old bogeyman of Democratic Party thought, loom larger in the liberal imagination than ever before. There is a new enthusiasm for regulation: as McKinsey discovered in the wake of the collapse of Lehman Brothers, CO_2 emissions, the financial sector and technology standards now require 'regulatory standards at a transnational level'. [1]

For years there has been a wider trend to big up the role of regulation in stimulating innovation. [2] The failure of the December 2009 Copenhagen summit on climate change, however, shows that regulation cannot be a force for technological progress.

LESSONS OF COPENHAGEN

Copenhagen doesn't just show the defects of United Nations diplomacy and the utopianism of McKinsey's call for international regulation. It also confirms that the focus for today's regulation is much more about targets, personal behaviour and Motherhood-and-Apple-Pie transparency than it is about innovation. The only piece of technology to make the headlines around Copenhagen was satellite surveillance of China's CO_2 emissions. Even the proposed transfer of Western energy technology worth $100bn to the South barely gained a mention.

Perhaps that's because, outside the ivory-tower world of international regulators, it's newly created Eastern technologies that are more likely to make a difference to energy supply than old Western technologies. And, in corporate innovation, are India's Suzlon (wind turbines) or China's Suntech (solar power) and BYD (all-electric cars) the products of regulation? Not much.

Since Copenhagen, Western commentators have vilified China and India as wrecking international regulation. [3] This shows how far the bureaucratic impulse has enveloped the Western mind. Agreements to cap and trade carbon emissions are thought more meritorious than real progress in the development of clean energy.

Copenhagen shows, finally, that a regulation is always a piece of paper 'cobbled together'. For that reason alone, regulation cannot really cohere popular backing for itself. Over climate change, governments have begged for campaigns to grow, and campaigns have clamoured for governments to go further. But Copenhagen mobilised no more than stage armies of protesters on the streets and in the conference hall.

A genuine movement for innovation will never be based on the demand for state regulation to be still broader or more exacting than it is.

REGULATIONS THAT HAVEN'T HELPED

Of course, there is regulation and regulation. When the world's manufacturers of mobile phones agreed that chargers should be standardised, who could disagree? [4] Yet continued restrictions on stem cell research in the US, and on genetically modified foods in the EU, benefit nobody. No serious harm to humans has been found to attach to either innovation.

Regulations growing out of custom and practice are one thing, but the regulatory enshrinement of monopoly power, as with AT&T in the post-war US, has done little for innovation. Similarly, in Britain, hopes that the state's procurements might encourage suppliers to break the mould have proved to be just that — hopes. [5]

GREETED BY POPULAR AND PROFESSIONAL ACCLAIM

Anyway, private sector compliance with state regulation is never guaranteed. From light bulbs through washing machines to government buildings and cars, governments offer sticks and carrots to make different stakeholders see sense about energy efficiency. Yet through what physical and social processes, exactly, does a legal piece of paper lead to world-beating innovations in these various fields? In the same way, the state and its quangos may set a target for 'Broadband Britain'; but it is the surrounding economic and political context, the technological possibilities, the attitude of employers and the attitude of employees that will determine the practical fate of particular regulations. [6]

Like innovation, regulation brings unexpected consequences. But the failures of regulation, its tendency to produce perverse results, its tendency to reinforce powerful interests — these things are much more given in regulation than they are in innovation. Right now, the world has too much of the wrong kind of regulation, and not enough of any kind of innovation.

Yes, the state should invest in basic research. But that's different from representing state regulation as a powerful force for technological progress — indeed, more often as the only game in town. Just because the state appears to enforce the solution of a particular problem doesn't mean that that's what actually happening. The record is one not just of market failure to innovate, but also of state failure to do the same. Just a glance at failed IT projects run by the British state shows this.
Today the state isn't interested in innovation, but in making the future

more predictable and more stable, in avoiding risks, restraining events, and imposing moral codes. By contrast serious innovators, whether they like it or not, tend to make things less predictable and less stable. They tend to take risks and let events take their course. It is not in their interest to dampen things down.

It might appear naïve to suggest that innovators put their trust in the people, but it is not so naïve as suggesting that they put their trust in regulators. 'Greeted by popular and professional acclaim' is a statement that, if true of any particular innovation, will better guarantee its future than any seal of approval made by the state. Innovators should trust governments to see their handiwork through as little as they trust markets.

The desire and energy to innovate come from neither the unconscious hand of the market, nor the restless malfeasance of the modern bureaucratic state.

They come from you, me, or someone yet more qualified.

References:

[1] Scott C Beardsley and others, 'Managing regulation in a new era', McKinsey Quarterly, 2009, Issue 1.

[2] See for example Stanford law professor Lawrence Lessig, 'Innovation, Regulation, and the Internet', The American Prospect, 30 November 2002, on < http://www.prospect.org/cs/articles?article=innovation_regulation_and_the_internet >. Here Lessig upheld the law-based license to use open code, the end-to-end norm of network architects, and the law-based right of access to US telephone networks as bringing great innovatory benefits — not least, the Internet. For a critique, see Gregor Claude, 'Goatherds in Pinstripes', Mute, 10 March 2002, on < http://www.metamute.org/en/Goatherds-in-Pinstripes >.

[3] See for example Joe Klein, '2010: The China Challenge', Time, 24 December 2009, on < http://swampland.blogs.time.com/2009/12/24/2010-the-china-challenge/?xid=rss-topstories&utm_source=feedburner&utm_medium=feed&utm_campaign=Feed%3A+time%2Ftopstories+%28TIME%3A+Top+Stories%29 > and Mark Lynas, 'How do I know China wrecked the Copenhagen deal? I was in the room', The Guardian, 22 December 2009, on < http://www.guardian.co.uk/environment/2009/dec/22/copenhagen-climate-change-mark-lynas >.

[4] See International Telecommunication Union, 'Universal phone charger standard approved', press release, 22 October 2009, on < http://www.itu.int/newsroom/press_releases/2009/49.html >.

[5] See Sir Peter Gershon, Making a Difference: Reducing Bureaucracy in Central Civil Government Procurement, Volume 2 – Main Report, Office of Government Commerce, December 2003, and Releasing resources to the front line, Independent Review of Public Sector Efficiency, July 2004, on < http://www.hm-treasury.gov.uk/d/efficiency_review120704.pdf >. For the Tories' more recent position on procurement and innovation, see 'Osborne calls for money for small businesses', News story, Conservatives.com, 28 October 2009, on < http://www.conservatives.com/News/News_stories/2008/10/Osborne_calls_for_money_for_small_businesses.aspx >. For Gershon, the 'innovation agenda' merely jostled with the green agenda, adult literacy, small and medium enterprises and black and minority ethnic businesses in 'trying to ride on the back of procurement'. See his 'Public Sector Efficiency – did the Gershon Review make a difference and what comes next?', eGov monitor, 13 November 2006, on < http://www.egovmonitor.com/node/8570/print >.

[6] On the likely weak take-up of next-generation broadband access in Britain, see 'When will we get superfast broadband?', Point Topic, November 2009, on < http://point-topic.com/content/dslanalysis/BBAngamaps091112.htm >.

#12
THINK GLOBAL, ACT GLOBAL

For global collaborations around innovation to succeed, and for global flows of science and technology <u>genuinely</u> to convert nation states into a secondary factor in innovation, innovation needs to be internationalist in thought and deed.

The innovator should aim to benefit the whole world, not any particular purse or nation. He or she should know about and uphold the achievements of innovators abroad, and oppose all attempts to pervert or stunt innovation there.

There is no such thing as Jewish physics, which is what the Nazis called Einstein's relativity theory. Nor, by themselves, do the Nazi origins of the coal-to-liquids Fischer-Tropsch process make it a redundant energy technology. Yes, Israeli universities are tainted by their involvement in military R&D — but exactly the same is true of universities everywhere. The direction and worth of scientific enquiry can be distorted by different political regimes (most notoriously, genetics under Joseph Stalin and immunology under Thabo Mbeki). But if a piece of science can withstand expert criticism and the classic test of falsifiability, then its benefits in technology and innovation are indivisible.

PLACE IS OVERRATED

The historical development of innovation has certainly occurred, at different times, in definite places. However, place is overrated as a source of innovations. The Green slogan 'think global, act local' reduces the scope for human action. Innovation means going beyond your immediate experience. In innovation, both ambition and action need to be unbounded and global.

Place has anyway burdened innovation for reasons that go beyond it. A wider culture values place, because it's seen as essential to that evanescent thing, a sense of belonging. Sadly, though, innovation cannot reinforce a sense of belonging. Even the most advanced, most social versions of Web 2.0 social networking do not guarantee that. If anything, innovation disrupts the old order. It prompts misgivings more than a sense of belonging.

Electronic maps of the local, whether on mobile devices, in cars, or on the street, have much to recommend them. The cult of the local is another matter. Locally grown and bought food, local services, cities and regions, decentralised sources of energy and local green spaces do not at all guarantee innovation.

Scientific and technological breakthroughs have very often occurred in different countries simultaneously. Likewise, real innovations have mostly had an international impact. The spirit of innovation is to find solutions that are universal, not just local.

THE SPACE FOR INNOVATION

Back in 1890, England's Alfred Marshall praised not the intrinsic creation of value through innovation, but the benefits firms gained extrinsically, from the amenities of a place: better climate, roads, water, drainage, newspapers, books, and better 'places of amusement and instruction'. [1] Then, left-leaning French sociologists of the 1970s, followed by Anglo-Saxon sympathisers in the 1980s, concluded that command over space was the key ingredient of power. [2] By 1990, returning to Marshall, Harvard professor Michael Porter could rally economics behind the idea that local conditions are what inspire innovation. [3]

In a striking piece of non-innovation, the doctrine that geographical clusters of local firms in the same industry form powerful sources of innovation still holds undiminished sway over city planners and academics. [4] The simple idea here is that proximity assists the exchange of tacit, or informal knowledge. But innovation isn't especially about informal knowledge; for to get things done with any timeliness or precision, the explicit sort of knowledge — written formulae, blueprints and the like — is much more vital. Nor, more fundamentally, is innovation about the exchange of existing ideas. Innovation depends on the development of new knowledge, not just its intimate transfer. [5]

Amending Porter's thesis, some hold that the long-distance geography and movement of people are the keys to innovation. Berkeley's AnnaLee Saxenian believes that Asian engineers migrating to Silicon Valley have formed entrepreneurial networks that have helped Asia, turning a brain drain into a 'brain circulation'. Chicago's Saskia Sassen contends that the financial innovation of the 1980s 'was decisively enabled' by 'an increasingly transnationalized subculture of mostly young financial professionals who were knowledgeable about the pertinent mathematics and computer software'. Toronto's Richard Florida proposes that, with innovation, 'only about two or three dozen places across the world make the cut' — because of 'the tendency of creative people to seek out and thrive in like-minded groups'. In a British mirroring of Florida's position, others say that innovation comes from the 'diversity dividend' in cities, or the commingling of different cultures. [6]

From Porter on, all these theories share a focus on the circulation of innovations, not their production. Thought, experiment, self-questioning, fierce debate, prototypes and budgets for R&D count for little. Instead, innovation is advanced by walking into local universities, watering holes and mosques, or by getting on to aeroplanes. Brilliant!

SLUMS AS AN EXAMPLE TO FOLLOW

Dogmas about the spatial origins of innovation reach a new low around innovation in urban form. Beginning with the concept of 'smart' or 'compact' growth, the city, so often lauded as a site for innovation, is attacked when found guilty of sprawl. [7] Thus, for London School of Economics professor Richard Burdett, Los Angeles must — as usual — be savaged for its two-hour commutes, and more densely populated, compact cities such as Hong Kong and Manhattan must be praised as 'inherently more sustainable places to live than the likes of Houston and Mexico City'. [8]

Where, though, is real compactness to be found? The answer is Dharavi, central Mumbai, where perhaps a million people live in just 223 hectares. Mumbai is the world's densest city; central Dharavi is perhaps six times denser than daytime Manhattan. [9] Is this, then, where proximity gives innovation a special dynamism?

From hip TV presenters to British royals, the broad answer given is yes. Kevin McCloud, UK broadcasting's high priest of residential design, insists that Dharavi, being car-free and lacking 'interest in material excess', is an economic miracle. [10] Likewise Prince Charles, contrasting Dharavi with what he calls 'a single monoculture of globalisation', says that it shows how 'economic advantages will arise from celebrating local assets and capitalising upon diversity' — and that communities like it may be 'best equipped to face the challenges that confront us' because they 'have a built-in resilience and genuinely durable ways of living'. [11]

So Dharavi, where privacy doesn't exist and open kilns are right outside front doors, is the model to follow. Backwardness is represented as forward thinking; the West has 'lessons to learn' (McCloud). Elsewhere, innovatory skyscrapers, which add to urban density, are nevertheless attacked as vain and hubristic. [12]

In fact, though, innovations come from people. Those people, moreover, operate in corporate or government buildings that happen to be situated in spread-out suburbs, or take the form of high-rise constructions.

Innovations won't come from slums, and there is nothing innovatory about housing five people to a room.

References:

[1] Alfred Marshall, <u>The Principles of Economics</u>, Macmillan, 1890, Book II, Chapter 2 – Wealth, on < http://socserv.mcmaster.ca/econ/ugcm/3ll3/marshall/prin/prinbk2 >.

[2] Henri Lefebvre, <u>La Production de L'espace</u>, Anthropos, 1974; Michel Foucault, <u>Surveiller et Punir</u> (1975), published in English as <u>Discipline and Punish: the Birth of the Prison</u>, Penguin Books, 1977; Pierre Bourdieu, <u>Outline of a Theory of Practice</u>, Cambridge University Press, 1977; David Harvey, <u>The Urbanization of Capital: Studies in the History and Theory of Capitalist Urbanization</u>, John Hopkins University Press, 1985, and <u>The Urban Experience</u>, Blackwell, 1989; Edward Soja, <u>Postmodern Geographies: the Reassertion of Space in Critical Social Theory</u>, Verso Books, 1989, Anthony Giddens, <u>The Consequences of Modernity</u>, Stanford University Press, 1990.

[3] Michael Porter, <u>The Competitive Advantage of Nations</u>, Macmillan, 1990.

[4] See for example Eurocities, 'WG Clusters Workplan 2010', on < http://www.eurocities.eu/uploads/load.php?file=2010_workplan-JDOD.pdf >, and articles in <u>Regional Studies</u>, November 2009.

[5] For a useful critique of cluster theory as it applies to the music industry, see Bas van Heur, 'The clustering of creative networks: between myth and reality', <u>Urban Studies</u>, Vol 46, Issue 8, July 2009.

[6] AnnaLee Saxenian, <u>The New Argonauts: Regional Advantage in a Global Economy</u>, Harvard University Press, 2006; Saskia Sassen, <u>Territory, Authority, Rights: From Medieval to Global Assemblages</u>, Princeton University Press (2006), updated edition, 2008, p361; Richard Florida, <u>Who's Your City? How the Creative Economy Is Making Where You Live the Most Important Decision of Your Life</u>, Basic Books, 2008, p248; Phil Wood and Charles Landry, <u>The Intercultural City: Planning For Diversity Advantage</u>, Earthscan, 2007. See also Stewart Brand, who believes that 'what drives a city's innovation engine' is 'its multitude of contrasts'. Brand, <u>Whole Earth Discipline: An Ecopragmatist Manifesto</u>, Viking Adult, 2009, p33.

[7] For the same old story, see Richard Rogers, 'Architecture for Sustainable Cities: London, Paris + The Compact City', speech to the Urban Age Istanbul Conference, November 2009, on < http://www.metacafe.com/watch/3841966/richard_rogers_architecture_for_sustainable_cities_london_paris_the_compact_city/ >. Critics of sprawl have been effectively answered by Robert Bruegman, <u>Sprawl: A Compact History</u>, University of Chicago Press, 2005.

[8] Ricky Burdett, 'Cities – Proposed Way Forward', <u>Futureagenda</u>, 10 October 2009, on < http://www.futureagenda.org/?author=8 >.

[9] See Katia Savchuk, Matias Echanove and Rahul Srivastava, quoting a survey by the Kamla Raheja Vidyanidhi Institute of Architecture, in 'Intro: lakhs of residents, billions of dollars', dharavi.organic, 25 February 2008, on < http://www.dharavi.org/A._Introduction >, cited in Sadhvi Sharma, 'Living in filth is no lifestyle choice', <u>spiked</u>, 10 February 2009, on < http://www.spiked-online.com/index.php/site/article/6197/ >.

[10] Kevin McCloud, 'Kevin McCloud on his trip to India', <u>The Daily Telegraph</u>, 8 January 2010, on < http://www.telegraph.co.uk/culture/tvandradio/6952436/Kevin-McCloud-on-his-trip-to-India.html >.

[11] 'Press Association reports foundation's conference "globalisation from the bottom up"', The Prince's Foundation for the Built Environment, 6 February 2009, on < http://www.princes-foundation.org/index.php?id=618 >, and Robert Booth, 'Charles declares Mumbai shanty town model for the world', <u>The Guardian</u>, 6 February 2009, on < http://www.guardian.co.uk/artanddesign/2009/feb/06/prince-charles-slum-comments >.

[12] Stephen Bayley, 'Burj Dubai: The new pinnacle of vanity', <u>The Daily Telegraph</u>, 5 January 2010, on < http://www.telegraph.co.uk/news/worldnews/middleeast/dubai/6934603/Burj-Dubai-The-new-pinnacle-of-vanity.html >.

www.bigpotatoes.org

#13
THE SPIRIT OF INNOVATION KNOWS NO LIMITS

Since 1972, the self-evident fact that there is only one Earth has been repeated like a mantra. [1] In 2008 the WWF introduced its state of the world report with the innovative observation that 'We have only one planet'. It went on to argue that 'by the mid-2030s we will need the equivalent of two planets to maintain our lifestyles,' and today insists that 'Humanity's demands exceed our planet's capacity to sustain us'. [2]

This account does little justice to the role of innovation, which mediates between human beings and the planet.

The resources that are limited today are not so much the Earth and nature, as human imagination, consciousness and daring. Already innovation has, in many people's minds, been reduced to an abstraction such as creating a more sustainable future. Today the precise and always unimpeachable goal of sustainability looms large not just in energy, transport, forestry and agriculture, but also at Wal-Mart, and in fields as varied as banking, commercial and residential property, packaging, design and IT. Even if climate catastrophe came tomorrow, it would be difficult to justify the narrowing of the scope for innovation that has taken place. Yet sustainability is now praised as a 'mother lode' of organisational and technological innovations, and it is said that 'smart' companies now treat it as innovation's new frontier. [3]

No doubt when Christopher Columbus set sail in 1492, despairing voices told him that there was 'only one Portugal'. And for the people of Haiti today, it is clear that there is not one Earth, but rather their own very special Hell and then, perhaps, the kind of Earths enjoyed by other people. For ourselves, we are confident that, in terms of what civilisation could achieve, there is more than one Earth available to mankind — even without space travel, which we strongly support.

By focusing for nearly 40 years on the same old finitude of the Earth, arguments for sustainability have often become directly hostile to innovation. Take the developing world. Climate change or not, it would fare better if it had better infrastructure. But because building such infrastructure would use resources and release greenhouse gases, this approach is discouraged. So to save the developing world from climate change, it should stay as it is.

This is no recipe for innovation.

A NARROWED SCOPE FOR INNOVATION: THE EXAMPLE OF CLIMATOLOGY

There can be no clearer example of the narrowed the scope for innovation than of climatology. No official statement on an innovative, low-carbon economy is complete without an opening declamation about climatology, and about the complete scientific consensus that is supposed to exist, within its varied disciplines, on the man-made origins of global warming.

This admiration for one branch of science, however, stands in sharp contrast with the feelings that surround science as a whole. Everywhere there are careless, instrumentalist and penny-pinching attitudes toward research in general, and especially toward basic research. Meanwhile, zealous scientific proponents of climate disaster such as James Hansen or James Lovelock have become celebrities. Indeed, the charisma of climatologists is now judged so great, the London Guardian feels

free to describe Rajendra Pachauri, chairman of the United Nations
Intergovernmental Panel on Climate Change, as 'a leading climate
scientist', which he is not.[4]

If climatology has become an idol, however, technology — even
technology for dealing with climate change — certainly has not. It is
true that one or two environmentalists have converted to nuclear power,
and that schemes for geo-engineering climate are not quite given all
the ridicule they once were. There are also plenty of boosters to found
for shares and jobs around 'greentech'. But in general technologies
for dealing with climate change are held too uncertain, too risky, too
costly and above all too slow to emerge. The end of the world, it's said,
is coming fast; so the right course, the 'low-hanging fruit' to be reached
for, is immediately turning things off, going vegetarian, not having more
babies, or insulating your loft. Long-term programmes of R&D are not
part of that agenda. [5]

RESOURCE DEPLETION AND THE DEPLETION OF THE HUMAN SPIRIT

Opponents of the technologies associated with resource depletion often
lead a larger and more silent kind of contempt for innovation today.
Methods of coal, gas and oil extraction are for them 'dirty' in more than
any technical sense. Technologies that might be thought renewable —
biofuels, hydroelectric power — are themselves thought to lead to the
depletion of food and water. Use the next generation of nuclear reactors
to desalinate seawater? That's out, too.

Grim forebodings about resource shortages now drown all calls for
innovation. In 2009 the chief scientific adviser to the British government
warned that, on top of dealing with climate change, population growth
and urbanisation in developing countries would by 2030 raise demand
for energy and food by 50 per cent, and demand for water by 30 per cent.
Humanity was headed for 'a perfect storm' in 2030,

'... because all of these things are operating on the same time frame... If
we don't address this, we can expect major destabilisation, an increase in
rioting and potentially significant problems with international migration,
as people move out to avoid food and water shortages'. [6]

Professor Sir John Beddington did go on, in a speech, to give a brief
mention of what he termed the 'enormous ingenuity' of mankind,
and also made a nod in favour of more investment in science and
technology. [7] In general, however, he followed today's fashionable,
simple, lurid and vulgar contrast between nature's limited supplies
and humanity's demand to loot those supplies and leave a mess behind.

In this framework innovation recedes into the background, any subtlety to economics disappears, and people, represented purely as voracious consumers, become a problem. [8] Those who speculate about a demographic time bomb of more old welfare recipients supported by fewer young wealth creators and taxpayers are oblivious to how robotics and IT might both increase productivity enough to deal with the issue, and at the same time give great help to older people in everyday life. Those who say that a UK population of 100 million by 2081 would make life 'intolerable' forget how, in China, millions of Shanghainese already manage to live together in skyscrapers. [9] Those who fear rapid growth in China's demand for coal and oil ignore how Chinese energy technologies are already ahead of America's. [10]

In a world where 3D nightmares are based on crude, 2D economics, it's now more vital than ever for people to hold out the possibility of what is today derided as a 'technical fix'. This does not mean that technology is an <u>independent variable</u>, solving all ills. It is Beddington's <u>human ingenuity</u> that creates technological solutions. Resolve, willpower, political vision and prioritising the <u>right</u> technology are the key factors to consider.

Yes, technological solutions themselves cause new problems. But on the whole, mankind has been able to solve those new problems too.

Those who are obsessed with resource depletion diminish what can be done with innovation. They turn innovation into a matter simply of survival. In so doing, they chain down the human spirit, which wants to see improvements.

WHY INNOVATION KNOWS NO END

In 1945, Vannevar Bush, director of the US Office of Scientific Research and Development, sent a report to Franklin Roosevelt that pronounced science to be 'the endless frontier'. [11] While, significantly, he noted that 'freedom of inquiry must be preserved under any plan for Government support of science', and took up a Roosevelt question on what the President had termed 'the war of science against disease', for Bush it was war, and what he called the 'ever continuing battle of techniques' surrounding war, that provided the main rationale for endless commitment to innovation.

Yet though innovation does demand endless commitment, that's not because of war. Rather, the human capacity for innovation and the human possibilities that emerge from it are infinite. Similarly, while fears of peak oil and peak gas are indeed overdone, there will never be a bound on human thought.

The frontiers of human enquiry have yet really to press up against the confines of the natural world. In a famous lecture given in 1959, the

American physicist Richard Feynman proclaimed: 'there's plenty of room at the bottom'. [12] What he meant was that, down at the level of atoms, enormous amounts of chemical, biological and other kinds of information can be and are carried in an exceedingly small space. More than 50 years later, there remains much to find out about and do in the atomic realm.

Of course, explorations at the nuclear level have given the world the Bomb, and objections now attach to every kind of experiment in the sub-micron world of nanotechnology. But if better understanding the nucleus can lead to the acceleration of radioactive decay, so understanding the atom can lead to new materials and new medicines. In the same way, humanity's grasp of the chemistry of CO^2 still has far to go. [13]

Done at an industrial scale, the recycling of waste also has far to go. The capture of CO^2 from the atmosphere is possible, and, in bulk, new transport fuels may one day come out of what is caught. But let it be noted that, to some closed minds, any kind of technological advance — even those based on astronomical forces — is suspect. The sunlight incident on the Earth is enormous, even in Britain, but the British government's Sustainable Development Commission has never campaigned for more R&D on solar power. Given the right locations and the right civil engineering, there is little limit to tidal power, but controversy still attends the construction of a barrage at the Severn, in the west of England. In principle there is little limit to wind power, either; but, all the same, a disturbing medical condition, described as Wind Turbine Syndrome, has emerged — based on a case series of 10 families allegedly affected. [14]

Natural limits exist. But right now naturalist prejudice tends to be just as powerful as natural limits, and much more inhibiting of innovation than they are.

MARKETS, STICKS, CARROTS AND NUDGES ARE NO SUBSTITUTE

Climate change, declared Lord Nicholas Stern in 2008, is 'the greatest market failure the world has ever seen'. Yet the main solutions proposed to deal with this failure are to do with the state imposing a market price on CO^2. This is not very innovative.

The fact is that climate science has itself benefited from technological innovation. Market mechanisms, like the sticks, carrots and nudges that are supposed to make human behaviour more environmentally minded, will never come up with new scientific equipment in the laboratory and in the field.

Stock markets for carbon, Green taxes and a more extensive labeling of consumer products do not amount to innovation. Instead of holding everyone a potential innovator, they convert everyone into a real perpetrator of environmental damage, lacking 'awareness' of climate change. Instead of finding new sources of value in the future, they concentrate on moral wrongdoing in the past.

Where, as with climate change, genuine environmental problems exist, innovation should never be underrated in its ability to deal with them. But innovation has a bigger agenda than simply the environment.

Innovation is open to anything and everything.

References:

[1] Barbara Ward and René Dubos, Only One Earth: The Care And Maintenance Of A Small Planet, WW Norton, 1972.

[2] WWF, Living Planet Report 2008, 29 October 2008, pp1, 2, on < http://assets.panda.org/downloads/living_planet_report_2008.pdf >, and WWF, 'Living Planet Report', 29 October 2008, on < http://www.panda.org/about_our_earth/all_publications/living_planet_report/ >.

[3] See for example Ram Nidumolu and others, 'Why sustainability is now the key driver of innovation', Harvard Business Review, September 2009.

[4] Randeep Ramesh, 'India "arrogant" to deny global warming link to melting glaciers', The Guardian, 9 November 2009, on < http://www.guardian.co.uk/environment/2009/nov/09/india-pachauri-climate-glaciers >.

[5] Hoping, somewhat forlornly, that 'It might be possible to predict, on the basis of spikes in patenting rates, when deployment will take off for each of the main types of clean technologies', some sages observe: 'Since irreversible climate change is already upon us, there isn't time to sit and wait years for great innovations to wend their way toward everyday use'. See Alex Rau and others, 'Can technology really save us from climate change?', Harvard Business Review, January 2010.

[6] Beddington, quoted in Ian Sample, 'World faces "perfect storm" of problems by 2030, chief scientist to warn', The Guardian, 18 March 2009, on < http://www.guardian.co.uk/science/2009/mar/18/perfect-storm-john-beddington-energy-food-climate >.

[7] Beddington, speech to a conference on sustainable development, 19 March 2009, on < http://www.govnet.co.uk/news/govnet/professor-sir-john-beddingtons-speech-at-sduk-09 >.

[8] Beddington himself, invoking the 18th century father of technology-free economic projections, asks: 'am I now a second Thomas Malthus?' He replies: 'Not quite', because, though he predicts a perfect storm of global problems in 2030, he professes himself 'reasonably optimistic'. Beddington, op cit.

[9] Alasdair Palmer, 'At this rate, life in Britain will be one big squash', The Daily Telegraph, 29 August 2009, on < http://www.telegraph.co.uk/comment/personal-view/6111574/At-this-rate-life-in-Britain-will-be-one-big-squash.html >.

[10] On America slipping behind China in energy, see John Doerr and Jeff Immelt, 'Falling behind on Green tech', The Washington Post, 3 August 2009, on < http://www.

washingtonpost.com/wp-dyn/content/article/2009/08/02/AR2009080201563.html >.

[11] <u>Science – The Endless Frontier</u>, Report to the President by Vannevar Bush, Director of the Office of Scientific Research and Development, July 1945, on < http://www.nsf.gov/about/history/vbush1945.htm >.

[12] Richard P Feynman, 'There's Plenty of Room at the Bottom: An Invitation to Enter a New Field of Physics', 29 December 1959, on < http://www.zyvex.com/nanotech/feynman.html >.

[13] George M Whitesides and George W Crabtree, 'Don't forget long-term fundamental research in energy', <u>Science</u>, Vol 315 No 5813, 9 February 2007.

[14] See Nina Pierpont, <u>Wind Turbine Syndrome: A Report on a Natural Experiment</u>, K-Selected Books, 2009, p27, on < http://www.windturbinesyndrome.com/wp-content/uploads/2009/10/WTS-sample-pages.pdf >. Pierpont believes that air pressure changes, noise and vibration coming from nearby wind turbines can lead to chest pulsations, internal vibration, tinnitus, headaches and ear fullness, as well as sleeplessness, deficits in concentration and memory, and physical symptoms of anxiety.

#14
BY, WITH AND FOR HUMANITY

The conception of innovation outlined in this Manifesto is humanistic. Science and technology are vital in this conception, but are merely means to an end — a higher human quality of life and societal progress. The more humanity innovates, the more quality of life can improve enough for more people to engage in innovation. That's a future worth striving for.

'Discontent', Oscar Wilde said, 'is the first step in the progress of a man or a nation'. [1] Today it is a mark of discontent to say that innovation confirms man's humanity, or to say that to be an innovator isn't the same as making your goals happiness, wellness and a low carbon footprint.

Innovation is done <u>by</u> human beings, and not by nature or by machines. Never a force for democracy in itself, innovation can nevertheless be assisted when it is done <u>with</u> the participation of more people. Finally, innovation is <u>for</u> humanity.

BY HUMANITY

Humans are unique, as a species, in their capacity to innovate. They are able to combine natural phenomena and past innovations to make a fresh round of innovations. They are able to identify problems and opportunities, analyse and interrogate them, conceive of, evaluate and rank possible solutions, and make these solutions happen in the real world.

In the late 16th century, the British poet Sir Philip Sidney gave a forthright defence of human beings. He wrote:

'Nature never set forth the Earth in so much tapestry as diverse poets have done; neither with so pleasant rivers, fruitful trees, sweet-smelling flowers, nor whatsoever else may make the too-much-loved Earth more lovely. Her world is brazen; the poets only deliver a golden.' [2]

Nature's world is brazen, but the innovations of poets, of human beings, are what distinguish us from nature. A bee may work in a hive, a beaver may build a dam, but they don't design things in the kind of conscious, articulate way that mankind does. They pass on no blueprints, and organise no schools.

Through its processes, nature produces new species and mechanisms. It can also often recover from the consequences of human error. But nature cannot innovate in the conscious manner of humanity. Mutation is a random process; innovation, though unpredictable, is a conscious one. Things can be learned from nature, but nature learns nothing itself.

In their history, human beings have invented different ideas of nature, just as they have invented different kinds of machines. But neither nature nor a machine can identify and value an innovation. Only human beings can do that.

WITH HUMANITY

Innovation in the shape of IT is not, by itself, democratic. It was not West German television that overturned the Berlin Wall, or text messages that overthrew Philippine President Joseph Estrada in 2001, just as it isn't Facebook that puts pressure on the regime in Iran today. Human beings, not IT and not innovation, are what bring about political change. Nevertheless, IT can help innovation become more catholic, if not more democratic, in its inputs.

As the New York journalist Jeff Howe has pointed out, mass use of the computer has contributed to everything from the design of T-shirts to the search for extra-terrestrial intelligence. That, however, does not amount to 'democratising' the means of production, as Howe maintains. [3] Two English authors, though they feel obliged to invoke what they call 'the age of consumer empowerment', are nearer the mark when they concede that, when surfing the intelligence of crowds, 'leaders should continue to lead'. [4]

Still, some kinds of innovation today are certainly conducted with a wide number of contributors. In its first two 72-hour sessions, held in 2006, IBM's InnovationJam brought together more than 150,000 employees, family members, universities, business partners and clients from 67 companies, who posted more than 46,000 ideas. IBM chief Sam Palmisano pledged $100m to invest in 10 businesses issuing from the exercise. [5] Similarly, before he left his job as CEO of Procter & Gamble, AG Lafley made it more open to outside ideas. [6]

These early openings to mass involvement in innovation have their drawbacks. The burgeoning and somewhat uncritical literature of 'open', mass collaboration in innovation outruns real results from it. [7] However, it is already clear that some kinds of innovation may be able to benefit from a broader range of participants than was possible in the past.

That's an additional merit of innovation today.

FOR HUMANITY

When they are not taking inspiration from slums, today's architects like to design luxury eco-homes for the very rich. But as the Russian architect Berthold Lubetkin famously and more usefully observed, 'Nothing is too good for ordinary people'. From Benjamin Franklin through PT Barnum to Norman Borlaug, the late father of the Green revolution, there is a long and contrasting tradition of universalism in innovation. Franklin's recent biographer observes that 'he declined to patent his famous inventions, and took pleasure in freely sharing his findings'. [8] For PT Barnum, the 19th century audience-conscious founder of American show business and 'Prince of Humbug' with a hundred faults, a human soul was 'not to be trifled with': it could 'inhabit the body of a Chinaman, a Turk, an Arab or a Hottentot', but was 'still an immortal spirit'. [9] Borlaug said that the destiny of world civilisation 'depends upon providing a decent standard of living for all mankind'. [10]

Innovations can and should be for everyone. During the Depression, Allen Lane, the audacious founder of Penguin Books in that era, wrote:

'There are many who despair at what they regard as the low level of people's intelligence. We, however, believed in the existence in this country of a vast reading public for intelligent books at a low price'. [11]

Reflecting on her participation in the 1951 Festival of Britain, the textile designer Lucienne Day notes that 'we wanted to design for everybody, not for the elite'. [12]

Soon, a simple test may be able to identify aggressive forms of prostate cancer right across the world's population. [13] Another simple eye test may detect Alzheimer's disease, again assisting millions of people. [14]

In innovation, these are the right ways to proceed.

CONCLUSION

In 1625, the philosopher Francis Bacon wrote an essay called <u>Of Superstition</u>. He held that the causes of superstition arose, in part, from what he called 'barbarous times, especially joined with calamities and disasters'. [15]

This Manifesto is issued because humanity faces such times now. It's a moment to catch one's breath, soberly reflect on what has been achieved by innovators in the past, and uphold what innovation could do in the future.

This Manifesto is a call to arms. Let all those who agree with most of it stand up and be counted.

References:

[1] Lord Illingworth, in Wilde, A Woman of No Importance, 1893. A version is on < http://www.gutenberg.org/dirs/etext97/awoni10.txt >.

[2] Sir Philip Sidney, in his Defence of Poetry. A version is on < http://www.gutenberg.org/dirs/etext99/dfncp10.txt >.

[3] Jeff Howe, Crowdsourcing: Why the Power of the Crowd Is Driving the Future of Business (2008), Three Rivers Press, 2009, Chapter 3.

[4] Martin Thomas and David Brain, Crowd Surfing: Surviving and Thriving in the Age of Consumer Empowerment, A&C Black Publishers, 2008, p7.

[5] 'IBM Invests $100 Million in Collaborative Innovation Ideas', press release, 14 November 2006, on < http://www-03.ibm.com/press/us/en/pressrelease/20605.wss >.

[6] See AG Lafley and Ram Charan, The Game-Changer: How You Can Drive Revenue and Profit Growth with Innovation, Crown Business, 2008.

[7] See for example Clay Shirky, Here Comes Everybody: The Power of Organizing Without Organizations, Penguin Press, 2008.

[8] Walter Isaacson, Benjamin Franklin: an American Life (2003), Simon & Schuster, 2004, p130.

[9] Barnum, speech to Congress, 26 May 1865, quoted in Arthur H Saxon, PT Barnum: the Legend and the Man, Columbia University Press, 1995, p221.

[10] Norman E Borlaug, 'The Green Revolution: Peace and Humanity', The Nobel Foundation, 1971.

[11] Allen Lane, 'Books for the million...', Left Review, 3:16, May 1938

[12] Day, interview by Sue MacGregor, 'The reunion – Festival of Britain', BBC Radio 4, 24 August 2003, on < http://www.bbc.co.uk/radio4/history/reunion/reunion5.shtml >; cited in Nico Macdonald, 'Practise, don't preach', Creative Review, September 2005.

[13] Arun Sreekumar and others, 'Metabolomic profiles delineate potential role for sarcosine in prostate cancer progression', Nature, Vol 457 No 7231, 12 February 2009, abstract on < http://www.nature.com/nature/journal/v457/n7231/abs/nature07762.html >.

[14] M F Cordeiro and others, 'Imaging multiple phases of neurodegeneration: a novel approach to assessing cell death in vivo', Cell Death and Disease, 14 January 2010, on < http://www.nature.com/cddis/journal/v1/n1/pdf/cddis20093a.pdf >.

[15] Bacon, 'On superstition', Essays, Civil and Moral, 1625, on < http://www.bartleby.com/3/1/17.html >.

Photo: The Stratford Box was the foundation for the new Stratford International Station which Eurostar trains now pass through from Paris en route to St Pancras International station

ABOUT THE AUTHORS

NORMAN LEWIS
Dr Norman Lewis is chief innovation officer and a managing partner of the pioneering European-based Enterprise 2.0 innovations group, Open-Knowledge. Until recently he was chief strategy officer of Wireless Grids Corporation, USA. Before joining WGC he was director of technology research for Orange UK, formerly the Home Division of France Telecom, where he led a highly successful innovation team. An expert on future consumer use of IT, he has written extensively about innovation, young people and social media, privacy and the future of communications. Until recently he was an executive board member of the MIT Communications Futures Programme, as well as chairman of the International Telecommunications Union's TELECOM Forum Programme Committee. He writes at Futures-Diagnosis.com.

NICO MACDONALD
Nico Macdonald is a writer, researcher and consultant interested in the social context of design, technology and innovation. His clients include the BBC and BT plc. Publications for which he writes include BBC News Online, the RSA Journal and The Register, and he is author of What is Web Design?. He chairs the Media Futures Conference and programmes the Innovation Forum and the Innovation Reading Circle. He is a Fellow of the RSA. See spy.co.uk.

ALAN PATRICK
Alan Patrick co-founded Broadsight after a career both consulting to, and working at, senior level for leading global multimedia companies such as the BBC, BT plc (OpenWorld and Ignite), AOL Time Warner, ntl and UPC. He has worked in the US, Europe, South Africa and the Far East. Broadsight specialises in providing strategic and system design consultancy for clients working with cutting edge digital broadband media, much of it real time and video. Prior to setting up Broadsight, Alan held positions as VP Corporate Development for Globix Corporation in New York, Head of Internet Business Development at BT plc, and advised widely on multimedia for a number of major TV and cable companies in his consulting career at McKinsey and PriceWaterhouseCoopers. He was involved in the design of broadband networks in the early days of their inception and has written several articles on the impact of lean operations on digital supply chains.
He writes at Broadstuff.com.

MARTYN PERKS

Martyn Perks is the founder of Thinking Apart. He is an expert in applying strategy, technology and marketing solutions for numerous start-ups, large-scale organisations and many small niche businesses. Martyn is a regular writer and speaker on design, innovation and technology. He writes for The Big Issue, spiked, New Media Age and Blueprint, and contributes a regular Digital Thought Leader column to NetImperative. He co-authored Winners and Losers in a Troubled Economy: How to Engage Customers Online to Gain Competitive Advantage (cScape Ltd, 2008). See thinkingapart.com.

MITCH SAVA

Mitchell Sava directs the Creative Industries iNet, an innovation fund and programme in the South West of England. Previously, Mitchell was senior advisor to NESTA, and continues to serve as an advisor in innovation and entrepreneurship to agencies across the the UK and Europe. In the US, he spent eight years as a strategist with Deloitte, where he launched the Innovation Well, the first innovation programme at a global consultancy. In 2001, he spun out OnRamp, a business accelerator serving start-ups and spin-outs of Fortune 500 firms. He served as a research fellow at the Center for Technology Assessment and Policy. Mitchell holds an MPA in innovation from Harvard University's Kennedy School of Government, an MSc in Technology Policy and Management, and a BSc in Computer Science. He is a member of the Institute of Directors and a Fellow of the RSA, where he leads its Glory of Failure project. He is also a founding director of OpenGov and Entre, a UK trade body for innovative entrepreneurs. See mitchsava.com.

JAMES WOUDHUYSEN

James Woudhuysen is a physics graduate, Professor of Forecasting and Innovation at De Montfort University, Leicester, and a member of the board of the Housing Forum. He writes for spiked, and occasionally broadcasts for You and Yours (BBC Radio 4). Helped install Britain's first computer-controlled car park, 1968; wrote about chemical weapons for The Economist, 1978; word processor instruction manual, 1983; multi-client study, e-commerce, 1988; proposal for Internet TV, 1993. Co-author, Why is construction so backward? (Wiley, 2004) and Energise! A future for energy innovation (Beautiful Books, 2009). See Woudhuysen.com.

Photo: Construction of a vent shaft underneath Corsica Street, north London. The shaft serves the tunnels through which the High Speed 1 line runs